VICTORIAN NEW ZEALANDERS

By JUNE A. WOOD

*An Elegant Family Album Descriptive Of
The Lives And Fortunes Of New Zealanders
Who Lived During The Glorious Reign
Of Our Late Beloved Queen-Empress
VICTORIA
To Whose Memory The Author
Respectfully Dedicates
This Book*

A.H. & A.W. REED

WELLINGTON SYDNEY LONDON

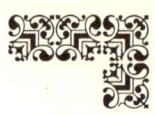

CONTENTS

Editor's Foreword	3
Introduction	5
Our Queen, God Bless Her!	8
Parlour and Pianoforte	14
Crinoline Kitchens	19
Fashions and Furbelows	23
Clothes and the Man	29
Garments for the Young	34
Pomatums and Pills	38
Tea-Parties, Calling and Other Etiquette	43
The Light Fantastic	46
Walking-Out and Weddings	49
Picnics, High Days and Holidays	54
Travel and Tourism	58
The Great Outdoors	66
The Entertainers	72
Words and Pictures	75
Church and People	78

First published 1974
A.H. & A.W. REED LTD
182 Wakefield Street, Wellington
51 Whiting Street, Artarmon, NSW 2064
11 Southampton Row, London WC1B 5HA
also
29 Dacre Street, Auckland
165 Cashel Street, Christchurch

© 1974 Estate of June Wood
ISBN 0 589 00844 7
Library of Congress Catalogue Card No. 73-91757

Set on IBM Composer by A.H. & A.W. Reed Ltd.
Printed by
Dai Nippon Printing Company (Hong Kong) Ltd.

EDITOR'S FOREWORD

In compiling this book June Wood was not intending a comprehensive survey of New Zealand life during Victoria's reign but rather to share her lively enjoyment in discovering and thinking about and discussing the apparent trivialities so often passed over by serious historians.

The space allotted did not allow her to discuss Pakeha-Maori relationships, so she chose to concentrate on Colonial Pakeha life under Victoria intending, I believe, to make the Victorian racial relationships the subject of her next book. But she did not live to complete the present book, for she died in hospital in August 1973.

By then she had completed the text and amassed a fine collection of illustrations, but illness overtook her before she could make a final selection of these and caption them and fit them to her text. These tasks were then undertaken by Barbara Richards, who has endeavoured to do them in the spirit that Mrs Wood herself would have brought to them.

The result is what we now see. I should go on to record two things about which Mrs Wood expressed anxiety when last we met. First, that a book of this size, covering so long a span of time and so many different levels of social life, must necessarily deal in wide generalisations, and for this she intended to apologise. I do this on her behalf.

Secondly, she feared that she might not be granted the time in which to thank, by name, the many friends in libraries and newspaper offices and elsewhere who had helped her in her work. She wished to assure all of them of her appreciation, but this I must do for her, with regret that her records do not enable me to do so in detail.

Finally, to record my own appreciation of a writer with whom it was a continuing delight to work. Our first contact was through her *Gold Trails of Otago* (1970) and we had a shared satisfaction in seeing it reprinted in 1971 and again in 1973. We worked even more closely on the present book, for by now she had moved from Dunedin to Wellington and we were able to discuss its development from month to month.

June Wood's enquiring mind, her devotion to accuracy, her gentle humour and warm sympathy with her subject, made her a most welcome and congenial friend and colleague. Her readers will share my regret that she did not live to give us more books such as this.

G.C.A.W.

*Lyttelton, 3 January 1883. The occasion is the opening of the graving dock and the first
ship in is the* Hurunui. *The great flood of immigrants came to New Zealand during the '70s.
In a single year, 1874-75, ninety-three ships arrived, carrying 31,785 passengers.*

They live among us yet who saw thee lie
A sleeping virgin, nursed by sea and sky.

From Musings in Maoriland *by New Zealand's ever-industrious laureate Thomas Bracken. The lady's name, indubitably, is "Zealandia".*

We greet you, stranger, to this land
Where slaves have never trod—
The breeze which sweeps our mountains
Is the Breath of Freedom's god.

Twenty-five years ago these lines of Thomas Bracken's might have been condemned out of hand as sentimental Victorian doggerel, but distance is beginning to lend enchantment to the long reign of Victoria, our late Queen-Empress.

It's not so long ago that words such as "hypocritical", "pompous", "sanctimonious" and "stuffy" conveyed twentieth-century New Zealand's attitude to the nineteenth. Those who were brought up in its closing years still remember with discomfort the restrictive clothes they were made to wear, the interminable Sundays, the narrow social customs, the muddy streets, the innumerable house-flies, the religious intolerance, the male dominance in public and private life.

These attitudes have undergone a remarkable change in recent years. Not only have Colonial houses and their furnishings come back into favour, but we sympathise more with the standards and the aspirations of the Victorians.

Hope was what led them to this country—hope for a better life materially, and for a freedom and independence vastly different from the rigid class structure and lack of opportunity prevailing in Victorian Britain. "Here I feel there is a comfortable prospect for our children, here they are respectable and respected, industrious, and as happy as is good for them," wrote Grace Hirst from New Plymouth in 1837.

It is all too easy to generalise about the New Zealand Victorians, because the one term has to cover the upper, middle and working classes, town and country, men and women, old and young, through sixty years of profound world-wide social, industrial and economic change. When the young queen came to the throne in 1837 this country as such was barely known in

Eighty days at sea between London and New Zealand, but not a particularly dangerous journey. According to an early writer: "Out of nearly 700 emigrant vessels, only two or three had been lost."

ship—and, for a long period of the long Victorian era, some North Island families lived in nightly terror of Maori uprisings.

Towndwellers could live in fear of starvation; the following letter, dated 1880, to the mayor, city council, and chairman and members of the Christchurch works committee, gives the idea: "Sir and Gentlemen, Your petitioners are the elderly men employed under the supervision of the City Surveyor at stone-breaking. In consequence of the carter being stopped in bringing supplies of boulders we are anticipating being thrown out of work. We are destitute of funds to keep us for any lengthened period, and we sincerely hope that you will endeavour to give us a continuation of work as before. And we hope that we may never be driven to the degrading necessity of seeking to be recipients of charitable aid. We remain, Gentlemen, your humble and obedient servants . . . ." The letter was signed by fifteen men, nine of whom could not sign their own names so "made their mark " instead.

the Old World, except to a handful of retired whalers and missionaries. But in 1901, when the old queen was laid to rest in the royal vault beside her beloved Prince Consort, the tally of her loyal Colonials in New Zealand had reached three quarters of a million and most of the city-dwellers were enjoying the sweet fruits of civilisation exemplified by railways, electric lighting, and the sanitary facilities available to townees all over the rest of the world. A Victorian New Zealander in the 1840s was living in conditions almost unrecognisably different from those obtaining for his urban grandchildren at the turn of the century. Yet in the remoter rural areas the way of life did not greatly change between the 1840s and 1901.

Throughout the reign a lack of good road communication, medical help, and of even the most primitive educational facilities made New Zealand back-country life full of material hard-

Stockwhips at the ready on the exterior wall of vertical board, the customary sack as doormat, a roof of wood shingles, and a biscuit-tin home for the brindle cat. Mrs Peake and family at Ohape, South Canterbury. (Canterbury Museum)

(Above and left) The photographers, professional and amateur, recorded much of our history. (Mrs B. Whiteside) (Nelson Museum)

The Devils' Books. Golden Bay. Nelson.

The Nelson studio of Theodore Bloch, circa 1870. (Alexander Turnbull Library)

The Colonial pioneers achieved many of their aims. By the end of the Queen's reign social legislation in New Zealand had begun to obliterate many of the longstanding social injustices of the Old World, and this country was being looked to as a place where the great liberal philosophies were being put into practice rather than being talked about as Utopian pipedreams.

On the one hand our Victorians were practical pioneers, in action on many fronts. On the other, they were still attached to quaint social shibboleths, and in reading the old letters and newspapers one is struck by what now seems naivety of social thought, as seen in two examples of mid-Victorian humour.

One is a riddle. *Q:* "What are the easiest weeds to get rid of?" *A:* "Widow's weeds, because if you say 'Wilt thou?' they wilt."

And: *Miss Jemima (age uncertain) to her maid:* "Wrinkles will come. Ah, dear me, they will." *Goodlooking maid:* "Don't be downcast, Miss, you know love is blind. Why, when Mr Williams come to call on you he often kisses me by mistake."

In a short survey of the Victorians it is impossible not to over-generalise, but I hope that this random collection of writing and pictures will add up to a fairly faithful impression of New Zealand's Victorians.

They were people, as we of the 1970s are people. And we may bear in mind that our own greatgrandchildren will be certain to find some of our antics and our mores as curious and as comical as we find some of those of our forbears.

Wellington
1973
June Wood

 **OUR QUEEN, GOD BLESS HER!**

Queen Victoria. Few if any New Zealand households were without a portrait of her on the parlour wall, on crockery and biscuit tins. (Alexander Turnbull Library)

Alexandrina Victoria, the portly and dignified queen who gazed down from the walls of most households in New Zealand from her Jubilee prints, had a significant personal influence on the manners and morals of our colonials.

When she came to the throne of England in 1837 as a young girl of eighteen she wrote in her diary: "I am sure that very few have more real goodwill and more real desire to do what is fit and right than I have." That desire remained with her to the end of her long life.

There was a considerable body of public opinion against the monarchy at the time of her accession because of the disreputable and unseemly manner in which her immediate predecessors had lived, but Victoria's formidable strength of character and insistence on the highest moral standards of others in public and private life gradually won her the respect of her subjects, particularly the growing middle class. But even the Queen was not immune from scandalous rumours—her surly, alcoholic but devoted Scottish manservant John Brown, it was whispered, enjoyed unusual privileges.

8

The Queen's serenity was echoed in the faces of the times. (Hocken Library)

The Queen's Christianity was a simple piety. She disliked being talked at about religion, and particularly disliked what she termed a "Sunday face". She was tolerant of other creeds, surprisingly free from class-consciousness, and had no patience with the colour bar or those officials who supported it ("snobbish and vulgar, overbearing and offensive behaviour"). On the other hand she considered the agitation for women's rights to be "wicked madness". Victoria could enjoy a good joke on occasion, but she would signal icy disapproval of any humour that she felt out of place.

Her blissfully happy marriage to Prince Albert and the arrival of their nine children made her the patron saint of respectable family life, and this deep influence spread throughout her Empire and lasted well into the present century. New Zealand papers followed the Royal Family at home indulging in music, sketching, painting and deerstalking, and followed the court in its seasonal progress from London to Windsor, to Balmoral, Baden Baden and the Isle of Wight.

For many years after Albert's sudden death in 1862 the "Widow at Windsor" virtually retired from public life and her popularity began to decline. Her prime ministers appealed to her again and again to let her subjects see her, and eventually she began to appear again at public functions. The Royal Jubilee in 1887 celebrated her fifty years on the throne with a great display of pomp and ceremony including a resplendent gathering in London of civil and military representatives from all parts of her vast Empire. In far-away New Zealand the Jubilee was marked by banquets, fetes and school picnics, fervent with loyal rejoicing. Victoria's personal popularity had reached its zenith, and Britain herself was at her peak of world power and prestige.

The Queen's face must have been reproduced literally millions of times on medals and plates, cups and caketins, and the royal approval for any homely product was eagerly grasped by the advertisers: "Borwick's Baking Powder is recommended by the Queen's Private Baker, and patronised by Army and Navy. With Borwick's Baking Powder you can make bread without yeast—saves eggs and butter—makes Norfolk Dumplings to perfection—is invaluable in the bush—to be had at all respectable storekeepers," crowed a notice in the *Nelson Examiner* in 1866.

After Prince Albert's death in 1861, the Queen virtually retired from public life. In 1887 the Royal Jubilee heralded her return and, like every other New Zealand city and town, Nelson celebrated. (Tyree Collection, Nelson Museum)

At the Queen's death in 1901, public mourning was blended with private bewilderment. Only those of seventy or more years could remember a time when Victoria had not been on the throne; she had seemed immortal.

New Zealand's first royal visitor was the Queen's fourth child and second son, HRH the Duke of Edinburgh, representing his mother when he came to our country in 1869 as a young post-captain in HMS *Galatea.* There were great celebrations in Auckland when he landed and the citizens turned out in their thousands to catch a glimpse of him. The *Herald* noted: "When the Prince landed next morning the town was crowded with people. In one case we heard of thirty pounds being paid to view the procession from the front floor of a leading hotel. His Royal Highness was dressed in a plain frock coat over light tweed trousers. His eyes are blue and their expression rather contemplative than scrutinising."

A highlight was the performance by the Auckland Choral Society of Gounod's *Messe*

Solennelle and the *War March of the Priests*, with several of the ship's personnel augmenting the orchestra. The musical prince himself contributed a viola solo, but ran into some difficulty because "moisture of the fingers caused the strings to break". It was suggested that his nervousness in public was caused by his recently attempted assassination near Sydney by the Fenian, Henry James O'Farrell.

In Wellington the entertainment committee decided to let the Prince rid the people of Miramar of a legendary fierce boar, though a few farm pigs were also planted in the swamp, just in case. The Prince appeared, the beaters beat, and a frightened pig ran out and was duly shot by the royal gun. The press made a great tale of it and the citizens rejoiced. During the visit a grand ball was staged, lit by hundreds of lamps and candles.

All over the country, settlers travelled on foot, on horseback and in bullock drays, into the towns to sight the Queen's son. Tumultuous gaiety and

Metal sculpture in the Victorian manner. This urban candelabra dispensed gaslight from on high and water below—for man as well as beast. At the intersection of Hardy and Trafalgar Streets, Nelson. (Tyree Collection, Nelson Museum)

Prince Alfred, Duke of Edinburgh, Victoria's second son, visited New Zealand in 1869. Loyal citizens await him at Lyttelton. (Canterbury Museum)

In 1875, His Lordship's Larder and Luncheon Rooms was dispensing wines and beer as well as food in Lichfield Street, Christchurch. (Canterbury Museum)

lavish hospitality were the order of the day. At most places the Prince was taken for drives, at times handling the reins himself. Wellington produced four greys for the royal equipage, Nelson followed suit, Christchurch went one better with six jet-blacks, but Dunedin trumped this with no less than eight greys, driven by Ned Devine, the greatest whip of the coaching days.

Apart from this one royal visit, New Zealanders' thirst for royal occasions had to be satisfied with vice-royalty. The Governor's charming residence on the hill in Auckland was the centre of social life when Parliament was sitting, and in 1860 Mrs Jane Maria Atkinson wrote: "The weekly 'At Homes' at Government House during the sitting of the Assembly are very pleasant. You meet everyone worth knowing, and have excellent music in one room while there is dancing in another. Mrs Gore Brown [the Governor's wife] has weekly meetings in her drawing room for the practice of glees, madrigals and masses." The great Dr von Haast sang at one of these occasions, and his voice was "unexceptionable".

The General Assembly moved to Wellington in

A notable Canterbury pioneer was Dr A.C. Barker, a medical practitioner and amateur photographer who was also interested in aeronautics. With him are Captain Lawrence of the Charlotte Jane, *Miss Lawrence, and the Bishop family. (Canterbury Museum)*

Governor (1855-61) Thomas Gore Browne, was more successful on the battlefield and in the social salon than in dealing with politicians and Maori land. His wife held "very pleasant" weekly At Homes at Government House, Auckland. (Hocken Library)

1865, and that city's greatest social events became the Government House balls. In 1890 there was the usual reception of *débutantes* "on presentation", but to their bitter disappointment, no dancing—perhaps it was one of those ever-recurring economy years?

We may assume that there was plenty of social climbing at times, then as now, but the determinedly democratic New Zealanders laid down that any Honest John who wrote his name in the Visitors' Book at Government House should receive an invitation to a party. After the party one called and again wrote one's name in the Visitors' Book as a polite acknowledgment of the honour (and perhaps in the hope of receiving another invitation). The parties were democratic, but the dinners given by the Governor and his wife would be more exclusive occasions.

Wellington became the capital in 1865 and its political and social life blossomed. Manners Street is no wider today than it was then and the Duke of Edinburgh hotel did business on Willis Street corner until late 1973. (National Museum)

PARLOUR AND PIANOFORTE

There's nae place like ane's ain fireside,
In humble cot or ha';
There's naething like ane's ain fireside
When frosty winds do blaw.
Nae place can warm the heart sae weel,
If peace and love preside;
It's there a man feels like a man,
Wi' a' a father's pride.

James Barr

As a general rule, Father was the supremely dominant family figure in the last century. Wives humbly played second fiddle, but old letters show much love and touching concern between husband and wife—our Victorians were never afraid of expressing tender sentiments.

An abundant enjoyment in the everyday life of their large families also shines out of many of these old letters. But the strain of constant child-bearing put a great strain on the mother's health, and also of nursing as many as ten or twelve young through whooping cough, measles, scarlet fever, thrush, chicken-pox, mumps, and all the other infantile complaints. Only the wealthy could afford nursemaids, and medical treatment was primitive and costly—where any was available at all.

One young wife wrote that she had been married eight years, had had six children, and didn't wish to have any more; but she was only twenty-seven at the time, and that was probably not the end of her family. In local histories you find accounts of this kind from an early settler

George Clarke (1798-1875), who arrived in New Zealand as a missionary in 1824, was in charge of the Maori school at the CMS mission station at Kerikeri. Here, nearing his life's end, he typifies the Victorian patriarch, noble, old, but still a formidable figure. (Hocken Library)

A Canterbury family of children, Christmas 1894. Many New Zealand parents helped to populate the young country by producing twice this number—and more. (Canterbury Museum)

describing his boyhood life at Tawa Flat in the 1880s: "Large families were the order of the day, and I might mention there were the Greers 11, Hooks 16, Captain Taylor 11, Constable Ryan 10, W. Morgan 10, G. Morgan 16. These are just a few, so you will see how easy it was for us to get up a cricket or football team with which, with our local dance and nigger minstrels, we had some fun."

14

In every town or city of any size there flourished a Gentlemen's Club. The Otago Club of Dunedin, 1861, is obviously well patronised. (Hocken Library)

If among the prosperous in the cities, Father led a comfortable life. He would arrive home from business to be greeted by a loving spouse, with his velvet smoking jacket and hand-embroidered slippers, which had been warmed in front of the fire by eldest daughter. As he sat waiting for dinner the voices of his numerous brood playing and arguing probably drifted in on him, his residence not being as large as those in England where children were relegated to distant nurseries on the top floor. At dinner he would carve the joint and the remains would be sent out to the maids. In some families the children were not allowed to speak at table unless Father addressed them, but this would not have been general. After dinner he spent his evening by the fire reading or playing cards, or he might stroll out on a visit to the gentlemen's club, or perhaps take his wife to the theatre.

In this formidably-decorated bachelor room are (l. to r.) Robert Turnbull (founder of Turnbull & Jones, Electrical engineers), E.F. Hadfield (son of Bishop Hadfield) and Alexander Turnbull, at the Turnbull house, Elibank, Bowen Street, Wellington. Alexander Turnbull bequeathed his later house and library to the nation. (Alexander Turnbull Library)

The study was usually an entirely male preserve. This example is at Kilbryde, Auckland.

15

But for most of the children in New Zealand home meant a warm kitchen and Mother presiding over the stove. Mrs C.E. Gilbert of Karamea recalls: "I can dimly remember sitting, as a small child, on the wide white-clayed hob of our big Colonial fireplace, with my little bare feet scarcely touching the floor. A fire was burning brightly, and over it hung two camp ovens, and a black iron kettle sang upon its bars. My mother sat in a low rocker crooning to my baby sister, while the firelight caught the silver gleams in her hair. On the hearth was the bread trough, with a rug thrown over it to conserve the heat and so help the dough to rise."

Mother and Father would consider themselves old in their thirties. In the earlier Victorian years young wives wore caps on their heads as a sign of being married, and as they grew older went resignedly into older and duller fashions. Many lost their figures, not only through constant child-bearing but also through the lavish quantities of food and drink they consumed during times of plenty.

Mum and Dad were parental names practically unknown until towards the end of the reign. Mum would be Mother, Mamma, plain Ma or The Mater; Dad, similarly, would be Father, Papa, The Pater—or, perhaps, The Guv'nor. Parents wielded great authority; they were given filial respect and were automatically turned to for advice, even by married sons and daughters. One family had a daughter, rather gay and flirtatious, who was married to a naval officer frequently away on duty at sea. Another man often came to visit her and played to her on his flute as she reclined on the *chaise-longue* in her crinoline dress. Her mother became so agitated that she took matters into her own hands and

Three young members of Dr A.C. Barker's family are captured for ever in a game of chess.

shipped her off to England before a terrible scandal brought shame on the whole family.

In grander houses the drawingroom, in humbler dwellings the parlour, was the centre for family gatherings and entertaining friends, and children were trained from an early age to contribute to the evenings by learning a poem by

Indoor games were never more popular than in Victorian times and the most frequently played card games were whist and euchre. This companionable quartet of the 1880s have found a sheltered corner out of doors—but cushions might have added to their comfort? (Alexander Turnbull Library)

Her china doll and handsome cane carriage would make her the envy of little girls in any age. An initial on a gold pin brooch, a carved ivory-bead necklace and a wristlet of gold chain with a heart-shaped lock are typically Victorian juvenile jewellery. (Alexander Turnbull Library)

A horse was the obvious present for a small Victorian boy, but he might be given a little steam locomotive when a few years older. (Canterbury Museum)

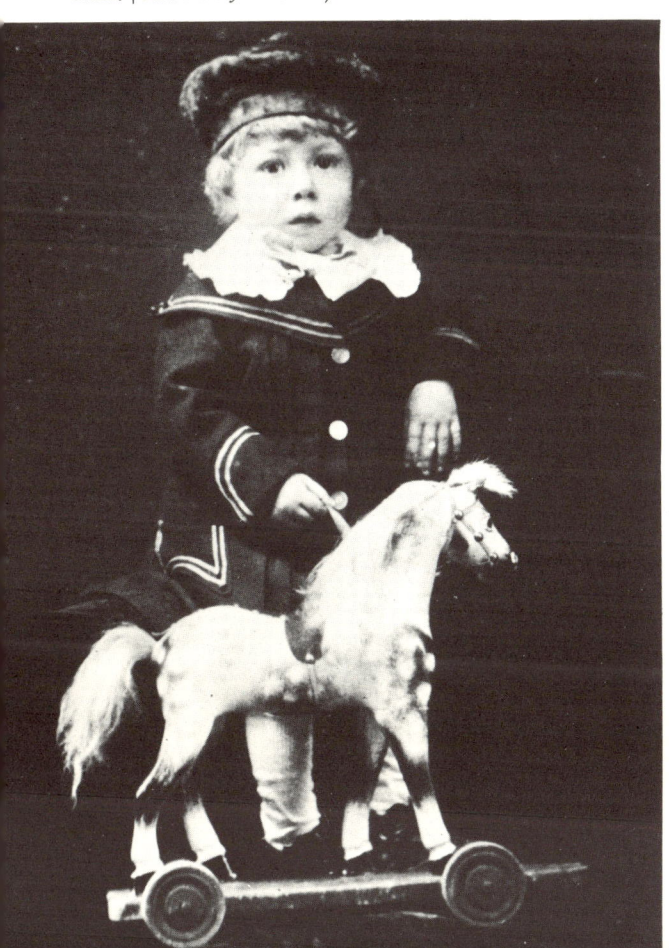

The oldest and most universal of all children's games, but after forty centuries of popularity one seldom sees it played these days. (Alexander Turnbull Library)

heart, perhaps *The Charge of the Light Brigade* for the boys, or for the girls verses by New Zealand's melancholy bard, Thomas Bracken.

> *She met me on the garden walk,*
> *Her bright eyes filled with mirth and glee,*
> *And listening to her prattling talk,*
> *My Childhood's days returned to me.*
> *"And don't you know my name?" she said—*
> *"Why, no," I answered, "We've not met*
> *Before, my charming little maid."*
> *Then she replied, "I'm Violet."*

Often home fun took the form of charades or acting plays or Dumb Crambo, for nobody minded dressing-up and being laughed at. Sometimes tableaux of scenes from literature would be staged: "Enid and Geraint"; "Home they brought her warrior dead"; "King Cophetua and the Beggar Maid". Amateur theatricals were always one of the features of country house parties such as those held at Birchwood station in Southland when Captain Gardner was the owner; his guests enjoyed racing, hunting and shooting by day, and dancing, cards and acting in the evenings.

The shops were stocked with a wonderful variety of indoor games—parlour croquet, bagatelle, draughts, chess and dominoes, and cribbage-boards, backgammon, and harmless dice games such as Royal Parcheesi, now long since forgotten. Whist and euchre flourished before auction bridge took their place, and bezique was a game for two hands. Gambling was for halfpenny stakes, but the family would more usually play for wax matches or, if your parents had brought them with them from Home, for little mother-of-pearl fishes, two inches long and exquisitely carved.

17

An Auckland drawingroom. Young ladies were expected to work diligently at both piano and needlework. What were commonplace accomplishments then are judged to be marvels of patience, skill and eyesight today. (Auckland Museum)

Often the children's card games tended to be educational, perhaps about people of far-off lands, or styles of architecture. But for adults and children alike, such games of course could never be played on Sundays.

As well as tackling the inevitable family darning and simple needlework and knitting, leisured ladies worked at crafts during evenings round the fire, and many samples of their crocheting, tapestry, berlin woolwork and embroidery have been handed down to their descendants. Miss Clough's in Dunedin was a little shop cluttered with goods to delight the heart of the modern hobbyist, and in the *Otago Daily Times*, in 1885, she was advertising: "Tam O'Shanter wools, knitted singlets, combinations, shawls, baby hoods, ladies' caps in great variety. Large assortment of traced and commenced needlework in plush, satin, crash, etc. Lace braid, new patterns, crochet braids, transfer patterns, macramé thread, tinsel and gold cord, fringes and laces; wax for flowers, purses, cigar and cigarette cases etc."

And in the *Napier Telegraph* of 1886 we see: "Miss Bacon, of the School of Art Needlework, Auckland, is in Napier for fourteen days giving instruction in Crystoleum, Poonah and Lustre Painting, Wax Flowers, Imperial Marble Work, Leather Work, Splash Work, Macramé and Point Lace, Crewel, Arrascene, etc." (Crystoleum was the process of transferring photos to glass and painting them with oil colours. Arrascene is a rich tapestry using silk and wool thread.) "By permission of the Colonial Secretary Miss Bacon will hold a GRAND ART UNION OF WORKS OF ART, comprising handpainted brackets, diapers, cushions, wax work, art needlework. Tickets 2s 6d."

The piano held many tender associations with jolly family choruses, and a daughter would hope to touch the heart of a future husband as she sat

Music was all-important in the Victorian home. This dedicated player has portraits of composers and performers on his wall—and one of Germany's Kaiser Wilhelm II. The light-switch dates this photo as after 1887, when Reefton became the first New Zealand centre to have electricity. (Alexander Turnbull Library)

and gracefully played and sang. Her fond suitor would be standing alertly by, ready to turn the pages for her (more people then than now could read music), admiring the glossy head and downcast eyes. Perhaps he'd be able to have a private word with Letitia while her mother went out to prepare the supper.

The young ladies of upper and middle-class families learned to read music and to play the piano and to sing, whether they had good voices or not. There was a social obligation on everyone to contribute to home entertainment and only the very young and the very old were entitled to enjoy the luxury of sitting back and watching. The songs were very sentimental, as the titles reveal—*My Bud In Heaven, The Heart Bow'd Down* and *Maying*—though ladies should avoid songs descriptive of masculine passion. Performers were advised by the etiquette books to sing or not to sing, not to complain about having a cold, or hint that they might perform only if further pressed.

Press extracts catch the mood of the early Victorian period: "New Music—*Sweet spirit, hear my prayer, I wait to hear thy sweet goodnight, Come where the moonbeams linger, Liquid gem* and—just published—*The Waikato Waltz*—composed and dedicated (by special permission) to Miss Cherry—by E. Bergman—Bandmaster of the 2nd Battalion, 18th Royal Irish Regiment. The title page is illustrated with a litho view of Ngaruawahia on the Waikato. Varty's, Auckland." (*New Zealand Herald*, 1864.)

"A young lady was playing the pianoforte with peculiar brilliancy of touch. A bystander bachelor exclaimed, 'I'd give the world for those fingers!' 'Perhaps you might get the whole hand for the asking,' said the young lady's mamma." (*The Globe*, Christchurch, 1874.)

"Mr Alfred Oakley—Having been instructed with the direction of the studies of some of our most talented ladies, he has determined upon settling here, and proposes reducing his terms to three guineas per quarter for Ladies and Gentlemen and for Children two guineas—Mr Darby's Music Warehouse." (*Nelson Examiner*, 1866.)

The piano was often the first luxury item to be bought for the New Zealand household and to possess one was not only a mark of the family's cultural standards but also of its prosperity. Country people especially enjoyed having such a sophisticated instrument in their home. In the towns spacious music shops flourished, and foreign names were an added attraction, as in this Wellington notice of 1875: "Music Warehouse—Salvatore Cimono begs to inform the public that he has opened a music warehouse in Willis St. . . . Having secured the services of a thorough tuner and repairer from one of the German manufacturers, he is prepared to undertake that all the tuning and repairing entrusted will be done in a satisfactory manner. Lessons given on the pianoforte, violin, cornopean etc. Great care will be taken with pupils that a correct system of fingering will be imparted." Hire purchase is no novelty; at about this time you could buy a piano on deferred payment with five per cent added to the cash price.

"Ill temper among the members of the household is often the result of absence of cheerful amusement in which all may join. One of the best antidotes is Music. A Piano or Harmonium is always a source of pleasure, and sometimes eventually of profit also—J. Grigg, Pollen St.," says the *Thames Evening Star* in 1879.

 # CRINOLINE KITCHENS

"The staple diet of the gold-diggers was damper and bacon, sometimes supplemented by birds and eels," says W.F. Heinz in *Bright Fine Gold*. Early backblocks settlers fared better than that; they understood the art of breadmaking and raised vegetables and poultry, but they must have got wonderfully tired of mutton from the camp oven.

Even as late as 1850 meat, curiously enough, was being imported—hams and bacon, kegs of tongues, casks of prime mess beef, salted pork in

Ornamental moulds in copper or tin were an essential component of an "elegant" kitchen.

barrels, salted or smoked Labrador salmon. Dry goods and preserves were also being imported, but the papers were advertising fruit-trees from Hobart Town and most families would soon be self-supporting in jams and preserves. Beer, biscuits and boots were among the first of the Colony's home manufactures.

Town and township-dwellers were of course more fortunate in the variety of foodstuffs, even in the earliest days, and fortunate too in the purity of what they could buy. In the 1850s the British medical journal *The Lancet* exposed a scandalous adulteration of processed foods in England: alum was being almost invariably added to bread to give weight and whiteness (and dyspepsia); chocolate was enriched with brickdust, milk with powdered chalk, dangerous colouring material such as arsenic derivatives was added to confectionery, and sulphuric acid to beer.

Not so in Auckland. Mr E. Waters, confectioner, advertises his conversation lozenges, "bird's eggs", carraway comfits, musk lozenges, coltsfoot rock, horehound candy, black almond toffy, matrimonial toffy, star-and-love rock, imitation strawberries etc., and goes on to quote a letter from J. Mazzini Tunny, Government Analyst: "To Mr E. Waters. Sir, I have made a very careful analysis of various samples of sweetmeats manufactured by you. I found they are free from all adultery (*sic*)". The fortunate Mr Tunny also sampled beer from every hotel in Auckland and found it pure and unadulterated.

The coal range—a huge leap forward in culinary equipment.

The early gas stove was a fearsome contrivance, viewed with dark suspicion by conservative cooks. This example is circa *1864.*

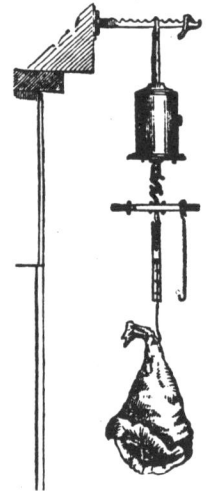

The bottle-jack or clockwork spit turned the joint slowly in front of the open fire. The notched bracket from which the spit is suspended allows the joint to be hung at the right distance from the heat.

The Victorian kitchen complex included, very often, a pantry for the storage of dry goods, a cool larder for perishables, and a scullery for washing up. The lastnamed might double up as a wash-house, which was more usually a detached building.

In the kitchen itself, cookery was at an interesting stage of development in the 1850s and 1860s. Before this, roasting was done on a clockwork- or hand-operated spit in front of an open fire, with pots for boiling operations suspended from hooks. A Dutch oven was a refinement of open roasting.

The 1850s saw the introduction of cast-iron ranges burning coal or wood, with hot-water tanks built in. Auckland opened the first gasworks in 1862, and by 1869 they were also operating in Wellington, Christchurch and Dunedin. The first gas ranges were primitive and sometimes dangerous, and gas cookery was regarded suspiciously by conservative cooks as being "unwholesome".

New Zealand cuisine was sturdily British throughout Victoria's reign (and for long after). Wholesome but over-rich, unimaginative, short on vitamins but not on calories, fussily overdecorated for festive occasions.

Meals were prodigious in quantity. In an averagely prosperous middle-class household, breakfast would include porridge followed by a cooked dish such as bacon and eggs, or cutlets, luncheon would usually be a full three-course affair with soup, meat and vegetables and a pudding or fruit. Dinner, even if only for the family, would include soup, fish or entrée, a joint and vegetables, and a pudding followed by a small savoury and/or fruit.

The result, in many cases, was a formidable obesity in both men and women, with gout and liver complaints unhappily prevalent. A young lady was not expected to show such a gross appetite but should only toy with her food; many a peckish damsel would enjoy a comfortable stodge an hour before dinner so that she could trifle with what was offering later at table.

Cookery books were at first imported, and Mrs Beeton's *Household Management* was a popular wedding present when it was first published in 1861. Battered copies of the early editions are still treasured in many New Zealand households.

Beeton is unfairly alleged nowadays to be terribly extravagant with materials but a closer look at her "Take a dozen eggs and a quart of cream" and so on shows that she's talking of a dinnerparty for fourteen persons. And while her menus for entertaining are elaborate, she prescribes much more modest fare for family consumption.

Mrs Beeton, in 1861, began a revolution in New Zealand kitchens. Despite this ornate titlepage the book contained simple and economical recipes well suited to a frugal menu.

Ornate silver or plated soup-tureens were de rigueur *in a gentleman's household—and a boring chore to polish.*

Victorian hostesses entertaining half a dozen guests and endeavouring to live up to her standards might offer them as a winter dinner:

First course: Palestine Soup; John Dory with Dutch Sauce; Fried Filleted Soles.

Entrées: Larded Fillets of Rabbits; Tendrons of Veal with Purée of Tomatoes.

Second course: Stewed Rump of Beef à la Jardinière; Roast Fowls; Boiled Ham.

Third course: Wild Ducks; Pain de Rhubarb; Orange Jelly; Meringues; Charlotte Russe; Almond Pudding; Fig Pudding. (The wild duck may look out of place among all that sweet stuff, but would be served in very small portions, as a savoury.)

Dessert and Ices

A Piha family on New Year's Day, 1885. The fluid they are enjoying may well have been a home-made wine, for winemaking was part of a good cook's qualifications. (Auckland Public Library)

But such gargantuan repasts were only for high social occasions. Beeton's recommended "Plain Family Dinners" are plain enough by today's standards and for a Tuesday night in winter she specifies: "Vegetable soup made with the liquor that the mutton was boiled in on Sunday; roast beef, yorkshire pudding, broccoli, potatoes; apple tart."

In her preface to the first edition she points out that "There is no more fruitful source of family discontent than a housewife's badly-cooked dinners and untidy ways", going on to warn her feminine readers that their menfolk's clubs, well-ordered taverns and dining-houses are in competition with the home table. In other words, she is repeating the old jingle:

> Ladies, don't start
> When I say that Love's dart
> Should be aimed at the stomach
> And not at the heart!

Indigenous cookbooks soon appeared, notably one published in Napier in 1887 which contains this message in its title—*Dainties: or, How to Please our Lords and Masters.* (Even in those pre-Lib days some ladies objected to that subtitle.) She recommends to a young niece, whose husband is getting bored with "poultice puddings", some desserts that will keep hot (he is notoriously late for meals), and suggests that leftover plum puddings and dumplings may be re-served stewed, baked or fried.

Coffee was at least as popular as tea for most of the period, losing ground in the 1890s which it recovered only after the Second World War. In the 1850s the Hirst family of New Plymouth refused to refresh their harvestworkers with beer but gave them coffee, lemon-squash and a one-shilling

daily bonus instead. As a result they got through much more work than the neighbouring, beer-supplying farmers.

The household week followed a traditional pattern. Monday was washing-day, Tuesday was for the ironing, Wednesdays and Thursdays were for general household chores such as the black

An Oamaru butcher's "boys" setting off on their rounds. Their calls were a welcome diversion in the housewife's morning. (Hocken Library)

22

job of cleaning out and polishing the range, Friday was a baking-day in preparation for the weekend. On went the aprons, sleeves were rolled and the range stoked up, for the tins must be filled and cold meat would be needed for Sunday-evening supper, so that servants (if any) and family could attend evening service without any serious fracture of the Fourth Commandment. This "full-tins" doctrine may date to the earliest days, when unexpected visitors were frequent, tired and hungry after long journeys, and today's continuing high standard of New Zealand home baking is quite clearly derived from this long and honourable tradition.

The Victorian kitchen was a friendly place and a spacious one by modern standards, though a shockingly hot one in summer. And, a very sociable place, a magnet for the children of the household when on safari for odds and ends if Cook was in an amiable mood. The back door was opened to a surprising sequence of visitors: suburban houses would be visited daily for orders by milkman, baker, butcher and grocer; the fish-monger, two or three times a week; bottle-collectors, rag-and-bone men, scissor-sharpeners, cane-chair menders, evangelists for strange religious sects, the organ-grinder and his monkey, collectors for charities, the coal merchant, tinkers to mend pots and pans, swaggers and simple beggars, perhaps even an occasional furtive, law-defying fortuneteller. A motley procession and a romantic one, but its passing is not to be regretted: many of these itinerant visitors lived on a pitiful pittance.

FASHIONS AND FURBELOWS

To describe in detail the changes in feminine apparel over fifty years of New Zealand fashion would require a very stout volume indeed, and in a short chapter one can only sketch the trends and quirks of the matter.

And, as throughout this book, it is impossible to avoid generalisations that must be at least to some degree misleading.

The clothes of the hardworking country house-wife and of the urban women of the working class were of necessity simple, cheap and func-tional, and had only a nodding acquaintance with high fashion. This does not imply that these ladies were indifferent to fashion; every woman had to have a "best dress", however humble, for church and other social occasions, and in the cruel custom of the period the pathetic attempts of maidservants to achieve fashionable finery could be the subject of a snobbish so-called humour.

If one couldn't afford fine clothes one could at least read about them; the newspapers carried tempting advertisements and ran fashion notes, and in 1880 a *New Zealand Times* advertiser was offering: *Young Ladies' Journal; Myra's Journal; Milliner and Dressmaker; Englishwomen's Maga-zine: Tailor and Cutter.*

Inevitably, the outward appearance of the fashionable women of the middle and upper classes changed radically, and several times, over so long a period. Our earliest ladies arrived in full and softly-gathered skirts that in the early 1850s were superseded by the first crinolines, which had the typical teacosy shape created by a liberal number of petticoats—up to *eight* of them—including a stiff one of linen and horsehair which

Maori attendants at early mission stations were expected to adopt European ideas. Rora Pare, painted at Pepepe by George French Angas in the mid-1840s, was described by him as "a regular vixen".

The bustle added a surprising fullness to the female figure from the late 1860s to the late 1880s.

The "full and softly gathered skirts" of the early 1850s. This and succeeding drawings are taken from fashionplates of the period concerned.

A silk gown of the 1870s.

Reception gown, circa 1878.

Fawn satin, 1880s.

The 1890s. The bustle has gone at last.

moulded the mass. In the middle 1850s the mass-produced "cage" crinoline, made of concentric steel hoops, came in—much lighter to wear and expanding the skirt to extravagant dimensions. (For a Government House ball in 1866 a fashionable dress would measure up to six yards round the hem.)

In the later 1860s, possibly because of the difficulty of leading a normal life in such monstrous sartorial surroundings, the shape became flattened in front with all the fullness behind, and the overskirt began to be hooked up for walking or croquet, this trend developing into the "bustle" which, with variations, lasted into the late 1880s.

Bodices during this time came to the base of the neck, or a little lower, with a long sloping shoulderline for day wear.

By the late 1880s the bustle had subsided to a mere pad, and interest began to be concentrated on the bodice and sleeves, which became fuller on the shoulder until in 1895 they had assumed an exaggerated leg-of-mutton outline. The high neckline persisted, with elaborate lapels and drapings so that the top of the body appeared to have tremendous bulk. Below this the waist was corseted to an agonising slimness, and the skirt fitted smoothly over the hips and down to the instep with only a token fullness at the back.

The firm rigidity of the Victorian feminine outline was preserved, of course, by means of the corset, or stays, which were made of fine woven material heavily reinforced by whalebone, and with laces which could be pulled so tight as to distort the natural figure into the fashionable double-eggcup shape.

A seventeen-inch waist was the ideal, and though this can seldom have been achieved in practice, some women endured agonies of tight-lacing in the attempt. The unnatural constriction may explain why fashionable ladies went into a swoon at the slightest provocation and had to be resuscitated with smelling-salts, or a burning feather waved under the nostrils.

Pressure from enlightened medical men and the "New Women" of the 1890s eventually restored the female shape to something nearer the natural outline.

The 1890s are interesting because fashion had to conform to new social trends. Tennis and cycling were demanding more functional costume, and "respectable" women were beginning to take jobs; women's suffrage and emancipation were in the air, the new sewing machines were encouraging thrifty women to make the simpler kinds of clothing, and there was a general swing towards the wearing of smart tailormades of rather masculine cut for day wear, though evening dresses were still ultra-feminine.

Underclothes were, of course, "unmentionables" and were advertised very discreetly. Most garments surviving in our museums today are entirely in white, with perhaps a daring modicum of broderie anglais, though a *Nelson Examiner* advertisement of 1866 makes an intriguing mention of "scarlet merino stays".

24

In 1885 Great-grandma would have donned, first, a chemise and drawers tied with tapes, then her corset. Next, a camisole or corset-cover; at least two petticoats (in winter one would be flannel); then a bustle-cage of some kind; then a best petticoat, gored and shaped to fit over the bustle, and lastly stockings, of pearl or black silk or black or grey merino or cotton. Only then would she be ready to put her dress on.

For outdoors she would have boots of cloth or cordovan leather, double-soled and galoshed for winter wear. Shoes were for indoors—of prunella, or morocco, or kid or patent leather for day wear, black or white satin for the evening. In the 1850s Charlotte Godley wrote from Christchurch: "Mrs Russell danced forty times and wore out the only tidy pair of thin boots she had (you cannot realise what a misfortune that is here)"— suggesting that, then as now, it wasn't always possible to get your chosen size and style at short notice.

A Palmerston North boot-and-shoe man in 1883 advertised his wares in lyric strain:

Let poets sing what theme they choose,
I sing about my Boots and Shoes.
Some sing of ladies, dark or fair,
Of golden locks or raven hair.
Give me the feet, then (I'm all there)
To fit them with a lovely pair—etc, etc.

So enterprising a salesman should have been rewarded with brisk trade, but the wiles of such tradesmen brought satirical comment from *Dunedin Punch* in 1866: "Mr Smallcash complains of a counter-feat by which his beloved Maria was lately victimised in the most (hea)rtless manner. That amiable but weakminded woman went into a draper's shop to purchase a reel of cotton and a yard of calico and came away with a 'lovely' new silk dress, a 'duck' of a bonnet, a 'bewitching' mantle, six 'elegant' French frilled nightcaps—and an empty purse. Ladies, beware!''

Glove and haberdashery department, Iredale's shop, Auckland 1897. Lady customers sat down to their shopping in Victorian days.

Taking a final glance at the very early pioneer days, there's a touching quality about the wedding day of Ellen and Mary, two of Bishop Harper's daughters. They and a sister shared a little attic room with a sloping roof, their saddles slung over the rafters and on top of these their ball dresses, pinned up in sheets. The room was so tiny that when the wedding day came Mary had to stand on her bed to dress; then the two girls, in their wedding crinolines, carefully manoeuvred backwards down the attic ladder to join the family downstairs. They must have made a very pretty picture . . . .

We have mentioned the "New Woman"—this was the label given to the pioneers of women's

Tennis and cycling introduced practical fashions in the 1890s. Mr and Mrs A.D. Bell, Shag Valley station, 1893. (Hocken Library)

Domestic service and shop or factory work were the only openings for "uneducated" girls. Nursing—after a four-month course of instruction—was for the better educated such as these Otago ladies off to the South African War in 1900. (Hocken Library)

Until the Education Act of 1877 introduced free and compulsory education, about half of New Zealand's children attended church or private schools, and the others were taught at home by governesses or parents. Until 1903, secondary schooling was only for the privileged. (Auckland Public Library)

rights, which Wellington's *Evening Post* satirised in 1875 with the note: "A Woman's Right: A Right to a Husband—IF she can get one."

Male chauvinists strengthened their case by classing women as "the gentler sex" but this term was often belied by women who were left widows with a number of children to support and who were forced to plunge immediately into the role of provider. One hardworking Thorndon widow with nine children rose at 3 am to clean the Parliament buildings. She then hurried home to get the breakfast for her family, then out again to one or other of the large houses in Tinakori Road to do the washing, taking two of the younger children with her."

Writing novels was the answer to stocking the larder for Charlotte Evans, who had nine children and an improvident Irish husband. Others managed hotels and boardinghouses or tailoring shops, or took up more unusual occupations. In Napier, 1886: "Mrs Caro—Dentist—Mechanical and Operative—Clive Square." In Canterbury, 1878: "Madame Josephine, Professor of Phrenology and Astrology, may be consulted daily after 11 am at her residence, corner of Park Terrace and Chester St."

There must have been just as many really capable women in this country then as now, but the traditionalist view at the time was that a man was definitely superior to his mate, as this letter

Ladies' College, Nelson, 1889. The couple in the foreground have decided that the net is a mere impediment to enjoyable tennis. (Tyree Collection, Nelson Museum)

Where I went to College!

on Mixed Schools to the *Nelson Examiner* in 1866 suggests: "The presence of boys and girls in the same school under the superintendence of a judicious teacher has evidently the effect of stimulating both sexes in a way that could not be done were they instructed apart. The boys are put on their best behaviour and taught to cultivate feelings of gentleness and politeness by being brought into contact with pupils of the other sex, whilst the girls are stimulated to a greater amount of exertion and painstaking effort than would be their wont by the superior vigour and energy displayed by their sterner competitors in the career of learning." (Nelson was a pioneer province in the field of education.)

Though some of the women's magazines suggested that a modest young lady should not be inquisitive about her future husband's income, in the 1850s and 60s a woman's assets and earnings became legally her husband's, on marriage. Where substantial sums were at stake a marriage settlement would be negotiated to protect the girl's property and expectations, and legal wrangles over this would sometimes lead to sadly cancelled engagements.

Mrs Mary Muller was very aware of these inequalities and she wrote many articles on the subject, using a pen-name because her husband did not entirely agree with her ideas. She was the prime mover behind the passing of the several Married Women's Property Acts between 1860 and 1894, and was also a pioneer of the women's franchise movement in New Zealand. Associated with her in the long struggle for women's rights were Sir John Hall and Alfred Saunders who gradually changed the climate of public opinion.

The outbreak of the Maori Land Wars interrupted the education of many North Island country children, such as these. They had to rely upon the teaching abilities of parents, who had little spare time during these anxious days. A great number of them grew up without any education at all. (Alexander Turnbull Library)

The reasonable arguments of Mrs Katharine Sheppard, who organised the Suffrage Department of the Women's Christian Temperance Union, also helped the movement. Her associates in all the provinces were able and determined, and were far from being the "shrieking sisterhood" that some of their enemies called them.

Alcohol was then as much of a social problem as it is today, and in 1905 W. Sidney Smith in *The Women's Franchise Movement in New Zealand* wrote of these Victorian ladies: "From the outset those engaged in the liquor traffic saw in the enfranchisement of women a danger to their trade, and were not chary in using very questionable methods for frustrating it. On the other hand,

The first National Council of Women met in Christchurch in April 1896. Kate Sheppard (seated, centre) was the president. Among this distinguished group of women are Lady Stout, Ada Wells, Amey Daldy, Margaret Sievwright and Jessie Mackay (3rd from left, back row), poet and journalist, for whom PEN established a Memorial Award for Poetry in 1938. (Alexander Turnbull Library)

Women's Liberation in New Zealand began in the 1870s with their interest in the cause of temperance. The temperance societies frequently adopted gay uniforms such as those illustrated. (Wanganui Public Library)

there were numbers of good men and true who, by voice and man, heartily supported the courageous women who were working for this reform."

The Enfranchisement Act was brought before Parliament again and again, but there were always postponements and delaying tactics. Mr Smith goes on to report: "Dr Hodgkinson was lugubriously antagonistic; he said The Bible showed the proper position of women. He believed that this doctrine as to the rights of women came from below and not above. It was contrary to the constitution of Nature and the ordinance of God. Mr Fish implored the House to try and imagine the feelings of a man coming home tired and finding his parlour or drawingroom filled with a lot of noisy and declamatory women talking politics."

When the Bill was finally passed in 1893 none of these dire predictions was fulfilled, and in the next few years many social reforms connected with the family and with working conditions became law. Flowers and gay dresses made Election Days semi-festival occasions, instead of the rather sordid saturnalia of drinking, horseplay and rioting they had often been in the past. The derisive male chauvinism displayed by *Dunedin Punch* in 1865 was no doubt a little apprehensive:

Fellow Bar Girls—
. . . and seeing there is no male creature in the province fit to fill the Superintendental chair, and that those who have already sat in it have behaved like ancient imbeciles, and having outraged the feelings of society—

Women were given the vote in 1893. Seven years later they were recruited for voluntary military service to replace the New Zealand soldiers who went to the South African War. Here is the Greymouth Khaki Corps, forty-one strong, in 1900. (Hocken Library)

therefore do I, Polly Perkins, possessing youth, beauty, energy and intelligence, determine to fight your battle, my battle, and every woman's battle, by offering myself as candidate for the office largely held by Mr Harris, and if we are only true to each other, girls, and to our watchword "the free, full, independent rights of women", at the close of the election you will be delighted to find me, Polly Perkins, on top of the poll.—
—Polly Perkins

As might be expected, the theme of Women's Rights proved irresistible to Maoriland's laureate songster, Thomas Bracken. We have space to quote only one of his seven moving stanzas on the subject:

'Tis woman's right to be caressed
When love is in the spring,
And when affection's harvest comes,
Her right it is to bring
The garnered fruits of happiness
To cheer man's dreary way,
To smooth his rougher nature
And refine his coarser clay.

Returning to feminine dress—it is tempting to hark back and explore the infinite variety of shawls and feather boas; handbags, purses and reticules; parasols and umbrellas; trinkets, jewellery and chatelaines. But space and the reader's patience are growing short, and we must now attend to what those Lords of Creation, the Victorian men, were doing about *couture*.

 # CLOTHES AND THE MAN

If we think of the mid and late Victorian eras as rather drab it may be because these eras of Victorian masculine fashion, in comparison with those that preceded and followed them, were clumsy, colourless, and left so little choice to the individual.

Surely our mid-Victorian male must have deplored the passing of the earlier ornamental waistcoats that we see in the Canterbury Museum— lavender with wine sprigs, mulberry satin with pastel-shaded sprigs, and cream satin brocade? And the modish garments advertised in an Auckland paper of 1850: "Black Satin and Black Figured Satin Vests, French Fancy Satin, Brocade and Shawl-Pattern Waistcoats. Embroidered and Openworked Silk Braces and Opera Ties. Coloured Silk Stocks and Red Cravats. Gents' French Velvet Hats ... Dress and Half-dress Boots, Blucher Boots, Cloth Boots, Oxford Shoes, Dress Pumps, Walking Pumps, Carpet, Roan and Sheep Slippers."

These elegances were for the city dandy, swell or masher, with a comfortable income; for the working men who made up the great majority of the population there were: "Men's Moleskin and Doeskin Trousers; Red Woollen Shirts, Bleached and Grey Shirts, Regatta and Scotch Twill Shirts, Blue Serge Shirts. Blue and Stripe Guernseys, Turkey Red Handkerchiefs, Scarlet Comforters, Serge Drawers, Lambswool Pantaloons, Merino Vests and Waistcoats."

These notices suggest that the men of the early

The Victorian male was as sober in his dress as his wife was in her morals. Suits of heavy tweed or broadcloth were stiff and uncomfortable, but hard-wearing.

Colonial period were fairly colourfully garbed, but by the 1860s and thenceforward to the end of Victoria's reign suits were of muddy browns, greys and blues and made of heavy serges, tweeds and broadcloths which were wonderfully hard-wearing but so stiff and so heavily lined that they can't have responded to pressing—hence the baggy wrinkled look we see in so many of the old photographs. Trousers with a sharp crease belong to the later, Edwardian era.

In the warmer months the scene was a little brighter. In 1866 a Nelson outfitter is advertising: "Light Summer Clothing at reduced prices. Silk Coats, Alpaca Coats, Wild Linen Coats, Light Vests, Light Doe Trowsers. Fashionable Summer Boating Hats in Tuscan and Rice Straw."

Choosing a comfortable city husband of the 1870s as our target, let us invade his early-morning bedroom, where we find him clad in a white linen nightshirt reaching to the ankles and a stylish tasselled nightcap, white or in a kind of Fair-Isle pattern as sported by Sir John Cracroft Wilson (1808-81) of Canterbury.

He will put on vest and long drawers or perhaps "combinations", of cotton or wool depending on the season; then a white linen shirt with starched cuffs and a detachable starched collar, and a broad silk tie or stock of muted colour, perhaps pressing the former through a gold ring instead of knotting it; and finally a three-piece suit, possibly not greatly differing from what his greatgrandson is wearing today—men are a conservative lot—but if our hero is strictly conventional it will include a frock coat, not a jacket.

Not quite a Colonial squire but a passable New Zealand country gentleman. Check cap, jacket and weskit atop cord breeches and leather gaiters, a horse at the ready and the pleasurable antici-pation of the day ahead. (Alexander Turnbull Library)

Beards, Bowlers and Burns. Frock-coats, canes and watch-chains, for a formal occasion. Dunedin laid the foundation stone of the Burns Memorial that still dominates the Octagon. (Hocken Library)

He'll wind his bulky gold watch with a little key, unless it's one of the new models with a built-in winder, and will stow it in his waistcoat secured by a heavy gold chain from which may dangle a variety of little gold gewgaws—a masonic badge, his watch-key, a cigar-cutter, a seal engraved with the family crest, a little case for wax vestas.

If he's a Dunedin man he may have bought his footwear from yet another of these poetic bootmen:

> *The football men of Wellington*
> *The Otago team did meet,*
> *But through M'Fadden's famous Boots*
> *They suffered a defeat.*
> *A hint to Wellingtonians—*
> *If you come again to play,*
> *Be sure you get M'Fadden's Boots*
> *Or you will lose the day!*

"Hurrah for Otago. Best Quality and Lowest Prices at the Dark Stout Man's Glasgow and Londonderry Boot Store, George St. New Elastics put in."

When he leaves for the office the maidservant will have brushed and ironed our hero's black silk top hat to an exquisite glossiness—the bowler is not yet fashionable and cloth caps and deer-stalkers are for holiday wear—and she'll hand him his dogskin gloves and walking-stick or umbrella. If it's chilly, he'll take a heavy overcoat called an ulster, or a cloak-type tweed garment called an Inverness cape.

Let's hope he arrives at his office with his shining headgear unscathed, for these things may be vulnerable, as demonstrated by an 1878 letter to the Dunedin *Evening Star*:

Sir,

Larrikinism

Will you kindly spare room for a word of warning to certain High School boys?
I was coming up Rattray St. today, wearing a bell-topper, and found about thirty boys preparing to pelt all comers. Now, Sir, I forgive them that one hat. If they do it again I will simply go for them and there will be some heads split open.
Nobody supposes that the masters are unaware of this larrikinism; if they do not stop it, who can wonder that parents, whose sons are meant to be gentlemen, send their olive-branches to Christchurch?

I am etc.

Pugil.

Cookham House (John Switzer, prop.) sold Cookham Boots. Strelitz & Hart's tobacco shop was handy next door, the Dunedin Gas Light & Coke Company rented the top floor. All this in Dunedin, 1865. (Hocken Library)

Holiday wear will be a tweed Norfolk jacket with matching knickerbockers buttoning below the knee, woollen stockings or leather gaiters and stout boots, a woollen sweater or cardigan possibly replacing the waistcoat.

Writing on male hats, Charlotte Godley must have been one of the first to record the old gibe at Windy Wellington's expense: "The saying is in

For those in uniform, the choice of what to wear was never a problem. A variant of Royal Navy uniform was adopted by the Nelson Harbour Board for the pilots who brought ships to berth through a narrow channel, and took them safely to sea again. (Nelson Historical Society)

There were many variants of the popular "tall" hat. Only one man here is wearing the genuine belltopper, most of them are sporting bowlers or billycocks. Quasi-military styles were commonly worn by boys. (Wanganui Public Museum)

New Zealand that you may know a Wellington man by his always having his hand on his hat. A hat-cord would not do, it would only enable you to bear it safely from one point to another, your head would never be covered. Almost everyone wears a cap and the few who persist in round hats have them of a most curious form. Mr Fox, for instance, has always in front a wavy line of brim, which has evidently, after many struggles, succumbed to a continuous pinch from finger and thumb—and Mr Domett's would be considered a shabby one by any decently-dressed scarecrow."

Mrs Godley was writing in the early 1850s—the informal period before men's dress had become citified.

Outdoor workers, of course, dressed in practical terms—low cost and long wear were their criteria. They were as highly hat-conscious as their city cousins: "Men's Blue Cloth Caps, Folded and Navy Caps, Drab Thrasher Hats, and Jim Crow Hats, one shilling each."

Corduroy working trousers were commonly worn, as well as the popular off-white moleskins which, a Riverton man recalled, were hard to wash but of beautifully durable material: "I remember when coloured moles came in for Sunday wear, they looked fancy enough but had an awful smell." If working in wet or muddy conditions, the wearer would use bowyangs—leather laces tied below the knee—to keep the trouser cuffs clear of mud.

In the early days on the Taieri Plain the farmers wore blue tunic shirts opening right down the front and lined with silk and which, worn outside the trousers with a leather belt, were considered presentable enough for social occasions.

People of both sexes and all classes wore hats while on the street. A hatless person would have been conspicuous at any time during the nineteenth century. Cloth caps were most commonly worn by the working classes, and on sporting occasions by gentlemen. (Hocken Library)

The Bon Marché of Palmerston North, situated where the DIC are today, catered for both sexes. Tailoring, millinery and dressmaking offered to suit each customer's individual whim, and fabrics at four shillings a yard! An impossible dream! (Palmerston North Public Library)

One man who had recently arrived from Home struck a dilemma—whether to say goodbye to his sense of propriety and attend a church social in one of those blue shirts, or to run the risk of being stared at as an oddity in his formal swallow-tailed coat.

He solved his problem by wearing his dress suit with the blue shirt on top; if all were in blue shirts he would be like the rest, and if any were wearing evening dress he could slip off his blue shirt and be one of the *élite*.

Later in the century oldfashioned gentlemen were becoming uneasy. Slackness seemed to be creeping in. Youngsters were wearing bowlers rather than bell-toppers, and instead of wearing a proper tail-suit for dinner, or a sensible maroon velvet smoking-jacket, they were taking to a scandalous thing called a dinner-jacket; young cads were wearing washable celluloid collars and cuffs instead of starched linen—to save laundry bills, so it was alleged. And some young fools were even sleeping in pyjama suits.

Sartorial snobbery prevailed. No gentleman would be seen dead in a readymade or "reach-me-down" suit. Made-up ties were as bad. Watches, studs and cufflinks must be of plain gold, eighteen-carat or, if you're one of these dandies, a set of white or black pearl studs is permissible—but only if they're real pearls, my dear chap. Only cads and bounders wear imitations . . . .

And another queer thing—studs and cufflinks made of some new light metal called aluminium. What would they think of next? Still there was something to be said for Dr Jaeger's knitted drawers and combinations, surprisingly soft and warm.

The Teaching staff of the Devonport School, 1889, and enter the trilby hat, worn by Mr Second-from-left, seated. Very smart with your punch-patterned boots too. Is that a celluloid collar? You cad, sir!

The garments thought necessary for a small baby in Victorian times added up to a cumbersome and constricting number, and one can only hope that some New Zealand mothers used their good sense and left off a few of the petticoats in hot weather, but of this one can't be sure. One small infant who later came to New Zealand was taken through the newly-opened Suez Canal in 1870 so swaddled in cold-climate clothing by his nurse that, had it not been for the good sense and advice of an Indian lady, he would have succumbed to heat-stroke.

The small baby's main gown would be of fine white linen or cotton, with either puffed or plain sleeves and fine embroidery. Very-best gowns and christening gowns were very long, so that the lace insertions and tuckings showed to advantage when the baby was carried proudly in his mother's arms. About the age when infants were able to sit up they were put into shortened dresses that came just below the knee. The safety pin, not invented until 1878, was enthusiastically welcomed in the nursery.

Typical garments offered for sale in Auckland in 1850 were: "Infants' worked Frocks and Cambric caps; Long robes and frocks; Stays, German stomachers and comforters; braided cashmere hoods and cloaks; worsted boots, gaiters and bootakins."

Up to the age of three, boys and girls alike wore little frocks and jackets made from wool, silk, poplin or velvet, with embroidered collars, flounces and so on, more or less following the adult feminine modes of the time. Much use was made of cashmere, which figured so prominently in the clothing of last century—a beautifully fine, soft woollen, either plain or printed. The head-gear would be soft gathered bonnets with ribbons for girls, and for little boys hats of felt or straw with ribbons or feathers. Charlotte Godley wrote of her little son aged three in the hot summer days in Canterbury: "Little Arthur says send my love and I'm picking gooseberries, and nothing he has on but his smocked frock."

It is interesting to compare the photographs of adult women with those of girls at any one year of the last century. The general lines are very similar, with very full skirts, longwaisted effects, and trimmings such as pleatings, plastrons, sashes or bows. But the girls' skirts are much shorter, and the younger girls' embroidered drawers sometimes peep beneath the hem of the dress.

Looking back at their Victorian childhood women tended to remember the scratchiness of stiffly starched petticoats. On the other hand they enjoyed dressing like their elders, and one woman remembers walking self-consciously to church in a new dress which had a small pad at the back like a bustle. Grace Hirst wrote from New Plymouth in 1863 of her grandchildren aged eight, off to school: "The cousins Margaret and Grace, they both wear crinolines and drawers."

"Babies Photographed. W. Davis, having just returned from England, is now prepared to take vignette portraits of young children or babies, in a very superior manner by Scaif's Pistol Camera, expressly invented for instantaneous photography . . . ." (Berry Collection Alexander Turnbull Library)

(Above, left and below)
The studio photographer was in
his first heyday in the 1870s.
Dresses were customary for boys
as well as for girls, and mothers
were fully conscious of the
importance of the occasion.
(Harding Denton Collection,
Alexander Turnbull Library)
(Canterbury Museum)
(Alexander Turnbull Library)

Girls were dressed in much the same style as their mothers, except that skirts were shorter. Pleatings were frequently used as trimmings. (Hocken Library)

"The younger girls' embroidered drawers sometimes peep beneath the hem of the dress."

The graceful crinoline, 1865. The name originated from two Latin words meaning "a horsehair", and linen fabric, which was used to stiffen and spread the skirt. When enormous skirts became fashionable in the mid-nineteenth century, cages of steel or whalebone were worn to keep them spread. (Canterbury Museum)

Girls whose parents could not afford fashionable extras often improvised crinoline hoops out of supplejack vines. Helen Wilson wrote of her childhood in South Canterbury about 1885: "For school we wore dark dresses, with pinafores, usually white, embroidered or trimmed with colour. For a party, the fashion of the moment for flappers was a bright-coloured square, pinned on to those same school frocks. The summit, if you could achieve it, was a large coloured silk handkerchief. You pinned one corner with a brooch on the chest, tied two behind with ribbons, the fourth hung down in front. Most of us had to be content with cotton squares but, if one could encompass a hair ribbon to match the apron, that atoned for all deficiencies."

It would be fun to be able to turn back the clock and watch a group of girls off to a party in their brightly-coloured pelisses (coats) in velvet, plush or wool, trimmed with fur, with bonnets to match. Gay striped stockings and socks and winter gloves or mittens were also worn by children, and quite a variety of boots and shoes.

It was considered a sign of shameful poverty for children to run about without shoes or socks, but there was a shoe famine in Christchurch one year, and the freedom of running barefoot was happily remembered by the children of that epoch when they were older.

Up to the 1890s small boys up to the age of about seven were fated to wear feminine dresses, with little jackets perhaps in plaid or plain colours, usually with braid trimming, and drawers showing beneath. Fond mothers would weep a gentle tear when their small son was *breeched*, that is, promoted to his first trousers, at which time his long curls were shorn. But he may not have been too pleased with his first best suit, which was likely to have been influenced by *Little Lord Fauntleroy* (1866), a popular children's book by Mrs Hodgson Burnett, the illustrations for which depicted the rather effeminate little hero with fringe and long ringlets, and always dressed in a black velvet suit with Vandyke lace collar. (Modern psychology could be interesting on this subject.)

"For school we wore dark dresses, with pinafores, usually white . . ." wrote Helen Wilson of her schooldays in the 1880s.

Mamma and her son in the 1860s. Romantic backdrops of graceful trees and country estates, which were so frequently used by professional photographers, look out of place in a New Zealand studio. (Alexander Turnbull Library)

When the Queen's own children wore sailor suits every New Zealand mother worth her salt wanted them for her sons, too. They were still popular fifty years later.

In New Zealand older boys look reasonably comfortable as they pose for their photographs, their clothing based on adult fashions—long or just below the knee trousers, with variously shaped jackets, notably the very short Eton jacket, which the schoolboys referred to as a "bum-freezer". Sailor suits remained popular right past the turn of the century, and Charlotte Godley wrote in 1850 of " . . . a little nephew of the Captain's, about eight I suppose, but small, and dressed sailor-fashion".

Kirkcaldie & Stains advertised in the *Evening Post* in 1878: "Boys' Cossack, Cheltenham Norfolk, Alpine, Yachting and Knicker suits. Boys' white dress shirts, military and pleated fronts to button behind or front."

Boys were boys as far as footwear was concerned in those days, and prices were prices, for as one parent wrote to the paper, "I would rather pay ten shillings for English-made boots than pay eight shillings for New Zealand-made, which last only a couple of weeks after getting wet. Protection duty is too high!"

Both boys and girls of even moderately well-to-do but Victorianly thrifty parents might have to put up with the indignity of wearing their parents' or siblings' garments roughly cut down to size. And to the end and beyond of Victoria's reign poor children were pitifully scantily clad, barefoot, shivering and chilblain-plagued in frosty weather.

The Victorians were proud of the Queen's navy and army, and pride was reflected in the semi-military and naval styles favoured for boys' suits. (Canterbury Museum)

"Toes out of his boots again—the little beggar. Kicks his way to school every day—and by the look on his face you know he doesn't care tuppence. Bless him!" (Alexander Turnbull Library)

Over the sixty years 1840-99 there were several trends in hairstyles for men, which they followed whether they worked on the stock exchange, in the bush or on the railways. Until the early 1860s men wore their hair longish and were either clean-shaven or sported a variety of facial hair-styles as varied as those we see in the 1970s. Charlotte Godley remarked that at a ball "The gentlemen, except for some cases of a little super-abundance of ornamental planting about the face, were quite unexceptionable."

The Otago Early Settlers' Museum, where the walls are filled with large portraits of hirsute men and solemn women who gaze sternly down at the visitor, is an awesome place to visit. These people were just as human as we are but the formidable bushy beards behind which the men, young and old, disappeared in the 1860s gave them the appearance of the more disagreeable Old Testament prophets. A useful etiquette manual gave the following advice on eating with a beard: "Never allow butter, soup or other food to remain on your whiskers—use the serviette frequently." A useful refinement was the moustache cup, which had a built-in ledge for keeping your moustache out of the liquid whilst drinking tea.

Rowland's Macassar Oil was the fashionable hair-oil for men and they applied it liberally, making it necessary for chairs to be protected at the back with the white embroidered cloths still called "antimacassars".

"Odoriferous Golden Oil—for beautifying and promoting the growth of the hair. Possessing all

"An exchange of photographs with dear ones 'at home' who will, no doubt, be surprised to see us looking so civilised."

The Crimean War of 1853-56, when conditions made shaving impossible, made men's beards fashionable in the 1860s through to the end of the century. (Hocken Library)

the qualities requisite for removing from the roots of the hair that excess scurf which prevents the escape of the insensible perspiration and induces premature baldness. It imparts a glossy softness to the hair, has a fragrant perfume, and is perfectly free from any colouring matter whatever." Persuasive copywriting from *The New Zealander* in 1850.

Bear's Grease (in fact a vegetable oil) was one perfumed haircream or pomatum used by New Zealand's young swells and mashers, and barbers' saloons flourished on the sprucing-up of the male: "Professor Rowley—Having at considerable expense improved the interior of his premises, begs most respectfully to announce that he is prepared to polish off the exteriors of his patrons in the interior of his establishment. The traveller who sails from pole to pole may seek in vain for superior performances to those carried on by the inimitable Professor, who confidently asserts that he is the 'ne plus ultra' of his profession. Having received a consignment of Bay Rum he is prepared to beautify the complexion of his customers, and his Golden Hair Wash can now be obtained. Near Swinburne Hotel." So says the *Wellington Independent* in 1860.

One school committee down south felt they had to dismiss one of their men teachers because the scent he used was too strong; but they were no better off when they replaced him with a lively young man from the university who was found drunk while in charge of a classroom.

From the early days when centre partings and smoothly drawn back styles were fashionable for women, the advertisements show that the shops stocked a variety of false hairpieces: "Wigs, Ringlets, Fronts, Braids, and Plaits on the improved principle, also Superior Perfumery, Hair, Nail and Flesh brushes, Tortoiseshell side-combs, Ivory tooth-combs, braid and dressing combs, powder puffs and boxes." (*Evening Post*, 1850.)

Milady in the 1870s and 80s was wearing very elaborate coiffures with pads, coils and switches added, curlers being used for the fringe. In the

A lady of fashion, who used tortoiseshell combs in her hair, rags to make ringlets, ostrich feathers for hats, wore Mamma's cameo brooch, carried a parasol, had the "vapours" when the weather was warm or her waist too tightly laced, and wept over East Lynne, *the immensely popular novel by Mrs Henry Wood.*

As the hardships of the pioneering days began to ease, and a "good strong female servant" could be hired for twenty-five pounds a year, women had more time to spend on fashionable hairstyles. Young "toffs" were adopting centre partings and using Macassar Oil. (Hocken Library)

evening flowers, ribbons or tiny hats were perched on top. Before retiring to bed it was a relief to "let down one's back hair" and to exchange gossip with a female friend until the gentlemen had finished with their brandy-and-seltzer and cigars. The phrase lives on.

"HAIR—Tresses of Hair, Plaits, Coils, Fringes, Wigs, Scalps, Fronts and Braids. The largest stock in the colonies. Suitable for young, middleaged or elderly ladies. Frederick J. Price—Grand Hotel Hair-cutting Rooms." (*Otago Daily Times*, 1885.)

A spirit-lamp, curling-tongs and curlpapers would be familiar objects on the humblest of dressingtables, and if they were used too enthusiastically there would be cries of dismay and a strong smell of singed hair. Other dressingtable paraphernalia included things in crystal, silver and ivory that have survived to this day, though their

For those who could afford them, best dresses were made of silk. And for those who could not, a polished cotton called silkoline could be used. (Hocken Library)

Zealand Gazette, 1875: "Stolen from the person of William Watson, stevedore, of Lyttelton, in a brothel kept by Honoria Fitzgerald, corner of Barbadoes and Kilmore Streets, five £1 notes." Honoria may have welcomed this cost-free advertisement of her premises?

Young girls on their way to a dance would rub or pinch their cheeks to make them pink and pretty, and used other ploys, as the *New Zealand Graphic* suggested in 1890: "How to darken the eyebrows is a question I am frequently asked, and for this purpose there are means many and varied, although it goes without saying that the majority of these partake of dye, to which many ladies wisely object. Crayon dust or a properly prepared pencil answer for the time being, and another thing is burnt cork. Shape a cork with a damp knife until it is exactly in the form of a very sharp-pointed pencil, and burn it quite black in the gas rather than the fire."

Inevitably one got to the age where artifice was essential, and older women often used *papiers poudrés*, which were little paper leaves torn out of a folder and crushed to powder. From Japan came rouge in little gilt-paper booklets with water-

uses are long forgotten: buttonhooks, glove-stretchers, pomatum boxes and little "trees" on which to hang one's rings overnight.

Towards the end of the era the famed English professional beauties appeared, who were photographed as often as film and television stars are in these days and whose expression, stance, coiffure and clothing would be emulated by girls even in far-away New Zealand. Styles of beauty were discussed at great length in the papers and the *Evening Post* had for example a leading article about Mrs Lily Langtry, a society woman who became a famous actress and an idolised beauty, albeit a faintly scandalous one. But youthful beauty must always be described as *natural*; no one was game to condone a girl's use of powder and paint, which were the hallmarks of those unmentionable "creatures" who were by no means unknown in New Zealand's cities in Victorian days. Notice in Police section of *New*

With the increasing flamboyance of fashions came the surreptitious use of cosmetics. A lady of the age here portrayed would make up—a little—but never a girl of "marriageable age".

40

In 1880 there were approximately 400 medical practitioners in New Zealand for a population of around 500,000. Not all physicians were as handsomely turned out as Dr Townend of Christchurch. The country doctor would have to ride long journeys on horseback, swimming rivers, and sometimes camping out when darkness overtook him. For the conscientious pioneer doctor, life was harder than it was for the pioneer settler. (Christchurch Star)

colour carmine blocks, ready to apply to lips and cheeks with a moistened brush. A dab over of rice-powder or fuller's earth on a swansdown puff completed the illusion.

The ladies of Auckland had their problems. One of them wrote to the *Herald* in the 1880s: "Sir—The dust nuisance is worse than ever. Really, Mr Editor, I never saw any place the equal of Auckland for the amount of petty torment to which the inhabitants are exposed. I should not be at all surprised if this place were made a sort of penal settlement for the more hardened characters in Purgatory, who would very soon be brought to their bearings if they were compelled to drink the drainings of cesspools, break their shins against obstructions in the darkness of night, have their food, eyes and throats filled on dry and windy days with finely powdered scoria, dirt and horse dung. I feel it severely, Mr Editor, for I am one of those ladies who, no longer young, are

driven to the use of paint, and I cannot afford to be continually wiping the dust from my face. (signed) Vermilion." The editor noted: "We have very little sympathy with ladies who paint, but for the sake of the public we think that, as soon as possible, steps should be taken to put an end to this nuisance."

Cleanliness was next to godliness, and those who weren't able to have their Saturday night bath in the kitchen in front of the fire, would go out for it. A Napier advertisement of 1886: "Mr E. Wigg having taken those Commodious Bath-rooms opposite the White Swan Brewery, hopes for the continuance of patronage awarded to his predecessors. Hot and Cold Baths, Plunge Bath, and Shower Bath, night and day. Cleanliness and attention are the main recommendation at these popular Baths. Special arrangements from 2 to 5 pm for Ladies."

Even today people looking round old attics may come on one of the little round cardboard boxes that contained the famous Holloway's Pills, which were a universal panacea of the last century and claimed to be a sovereign remedy for dozens of complaints. All rather sad, because many of the illnesses mentioned were in those days virtually incurable, including scrofula, which was sometimes a genteel term for venereal disease. Many popular painkillers and cough mixtures had a liberal lacing of alcohol and laudanum (an opium derivative). Other patent medicines were legion, and the newspapers ran several columns of advertisements on the main pages—Britain's Worm Powders, Pink Soothing Powders, Aperient Antibilious Pills, Chloroform Embrocation, Nervine, and so on.

Quack doctors set up their booths in public—as advertised in the Christchurch *Press* in 1879: "King of Pain—Prof. Scott's free entertainment in Cathedral Square last evening attracted a very large audience and the sales of medicine were brisk.

Invercargill, 1860-70. Homoeopathy was the treatment of disease by administering small doses of drugs which would produce the symptoms in a healthy person. The smallpox serum used today is based upon this principle. (Hocken Library)

In 1866 the morale of women in Nelson was boosted by this kind of wording: "Frampton's Pill of Health—For Females these pills are truly excellent, removing all obstruction, the distressing headache so prevalent with the sex, depression of spirits, dullness of sight, nervous affections, blotches, pimples and sallowness of the skin, and give a healthy, juvenile bloom to the complexion."

The men of Dunedin were being similarly assailed in 1885: "Decline of Man—Nervous Weakness, Dyspepsia, Impotence, Sexual Debility cured by Wells' Health Renewer—Druggist, K.P. & Co."

Spectacles were sometimes purchased from strange sources: "Having for years previous to entering into his business of Tobacconist, studied practically the adjustment and selection of spectacles to suit all sights, has just received a beautiful assortment of New Goods, extra quality in straw frames, light and strong, Coloured glasses for protection from sun and dust; eye glasses and common goggles. And will give free of charge a pair of spectacles to suit the sight of any person who cannot afford to pay for them." (*Daily Telegraph*, Napier, 1886.)

The citizens of Auckland were able to improve their scientific knowledge of the human body when a waxwork exhibition arrived: "The Royal Anatomical Museum—200 beautifully executed wax models illustrating every part of the human frame is now open at Mr Webb's Music Saloon, Fort St.—for Gentlemen adults only.—Descriptive lectures during the day—'Seek to know thyself. How beautifully and wonderfully we are made.'— The Museum will be opened for Ladies Only this night from 6 to 10 pm—A qualified Lady will be in attendance. All objectionable models removed." (*New Zealand Herald*, 1864.)

Homemade medicaments and cosmetics still held their own, however, and in the last year of Victoria's reign the new social craze of bicycling brought new facial hazards—and a remedy advertised in the *Canterbury Times*: "Cyclists. Cucumber Cream—This is capital with which to cleanse one's face after cycling. Take 2 rather ripe cucumbers and cut them in thin slices without peeling. Take a dish, and turn a plate bottom upwards in it. Heap the cucumber on it. Put another plate over. Stand a weight on it and leave all night. In the morning strain juice that has come away from the cucumber through coarse muslin. Melt in a basin 20 grains white wax, add to it 2 oz of the best of sweet almonds, then add the cucumber juice, and an ounce of rosewater, both of which should be slightly warmed. Beat the result with a silver spoon or fork, and when a whitish mass begins to form add 2 or 3 drops of any scent you like. After massaging the skin with the cream, wipe your face with a soft, clean rag, and then with a clean chamois leather."

Tobacconists sometimes sold spectacles, and always walking-sticks. Big wooden matches in big wooden boxes were 2d a box. Wax vestas could be bought in tins or small round cardboard boxes. Tobacco was 4s a pound. Woodbine cigarettes were ten for tuppence ha'penny and "ladies' cigarettes" were half-size and frequently perfumed. (Auckland Museum)

Mrs Buchanan's store on the corner of Mount Eden and Boston Roads, circa 1890. She sold almost everything, as was required of any good "corner store", looked after the mailbox, put the birdcage out whenever there was sunshine, and kept the trough filled with water for the horses. (Auckland Library)

Bicycling bought hazards to the complexion. These Christchurch ladies may well have used the Canterbury Times *Cucumber Cream. (Alexander Turnbull Library)*

Visiting cards kept in little mother-of-pearl or silver cases were all part and parcel of upper-class Victorian life and therefore essential to the socially-aspiring middle-class ladies in the towns. Every card had printed on it the afternoon that its owner was at home to callers, "Second Wednesday each month, 3 to 4 pm." Dressed very formally, complete with bonnet or hat, and gloves, they trudged for weary miles between houses, as usually there was no public transport. On arriving the guests would be greeted by a housemaid and led to the drawingroom, where they sat and conversed while tea was served with all the pleasant ritual of silver tea-service, fine china, wafer-thin bread-and-butter, a great variety of cakes, and the choicest current scandal. There were rigid rules about the right time to take your gloves off and put them on again, and a complex ritual of visiting-card etiquette that is far too complicated to be described in detail here.

Music might be played. "Now that it is too cold for tennis and garden parties, the musical afternoons are most pleasant—outside the cold and fog of a wintry afternoon, inside warmth, delicious tea, music and all the pleasant chit-chat that makes the charm of these re-unions," writes the Dunedin correspondent of the *New Zealand Graphic* in 1891.

Tea was taken in the parlour or, in grander houses, the drawing-room, a name abbreviated from withdrawing-room. Bamboo was in fashionable use for furniture (from 1880 onwards), and flowers and potted plants—especially the aspidistra of music hall fame—were sure to be there. An Auckland example. (Auckland Museum)

Christchurch circa 1865. Dr Barker and his family are playing croquet on a lawn that looks much too rough for match play. When guests called for tea they were often invited to play croquet, or tennis, or to join the family in making or listening to music. (Canterbury Museum)

Formal teaparties were an important part of the social life of Victorian women. When entertaining, the hostess invariably wore hat, cap or bonnet.

The elegance of colonial domestic architecture at its best in Mr Glasgow's house, Wakapuaka–a house for hospitality. (Tyree Collection, Nelson Museum)
near Nelson

Mrs Jane Maria Atkinson wrote from Taranaki in 1855 of a teaparty on a very grand scale: "On the first of this month Aunt Helen gave a tea *champêtre* at which sixty-five people were present. They assembled early in the afternoon and amused themselves as age and taste dictated in cricket, *Les Graces* (a French game played with two light sticks and a wicker ring), battledore and shuttle-cock, or strolling about the garden. A long table was made under the peach and mimosa trees near the house, at which Aunt and Hannah Smith presided dispensing tea and coffee. When sunset

and moonlight were mingling, the whole party adjourned to the house to dance."

Quite elaborate dinnerparties were given in the homes of the privileged. These required careful forethought on the part of the hostess, who would have an especially worrying time if she had a new cook or perhaps a gauche maid to train. In the diningroom each course would be served by one or perhaps two maids. Pre-dinner drinks were unheard-of, but at least two different wines would be served with the meal, differing types of glasses being essential for sherry, claret, hock, champagne, and port and brandy.

The women retired to the drawingroom at the end of the meal for a gossip, the hostess giving them the signal to depart, and the men stayed on at the table for the gossip and doubtful stories, with port, brandy and cigars. The sexes later joined up in the drawingroom for cards, dancing or music, with some of the gentlemen, perhaps, not entirely steady on their feet.

Fortunate families had an old family retainer, a semiretired "nanny" or housekeeper who would be glad to stay on with them for all her life and would take an almost parental interest in the grandchildren and even greatgrandchildren of the new generation, who would be brought to visit her and enjoined to treat her with great respect.

Country hospitality. The house may be primitive but flowers are growing and guests are made welcome. (Child Collection, Alexander Turnbull Library)

44

Tea traders' stand at the New Zealand and South Seas Exhibition, Dunedin, 1889. Tea was a precious commodity and was kept under lock and key, against theft by servants. Tea was 3s a pound, the equivalent of four days' wages for a maidservant. (Hocken Library)

But, in the main, the better-off housewives of the time were always lamenting the rapid turnover of servants—which is not surprising, as they were paid shockingly miserable wages, and expected to sleep in a poky little bedroom, often shared with another maid, and to work at least a six-day week, fourteen hours a day. There was a plentiful supply of replacements from the employment agencies, as a girl from a large family in the country found that to "go into service" in town was her only avenue of employment. Girls worked increasingly in shops towards the end of the century but wages were so low that town girls who could live at home usually filled these jobs, and respectable country parents were suspicious of city boarding establishments for their daughters.

From the pen of Mrs Randall in 1876: "My nurse is rather pretty, and seems a nice girl, but I never feel quite sure she tells the plain unvarnished truth, but I think I may assume she doesn't, seeing all I have learnt of human nature since I have been a householder ... A good deal of time is taken up in giving and receiving characters [testimonials] of servants, for myself and others, ordering dinner, replacing the brooms and shovels etc. that the servants break, and seeing that they do their work."

The other side of the picture, the maid's point of view, has not often been handed down but, it may be imagined, there must have been bad mistresses and good maids, and *vice versa*.

Fascinated by our many beautiful museum displays of typical Victorian drawingrooms we may feel that our grandparents enjoyed an enviable ease and elegance, and so they did—a favoured few of them—but by far the greater number lived in more modest comfort and with simpler social rituals.

Some, particularly in the remoter country areas, lived a harsh peasant life of bare subsistence: and in hard times a few of our Victorians, let it be remembered, starved to death.

Enter irate female servant: *Call yourself a lady and a Christian, and expect me to do the washing!"* (Dunedin Punch, 1865) (Hocken Library)

Polkas, galops, mazurkas, reels, waltzes, quadrilles, the Lancers, schottisches, Sir Roger de Coverley—all had their vogue in Victorian times and most of them were far more complex than the go-as-you-please dances of today. The Lancers, for example, had eight quite different "figures", with music of a different tempo for each figure culminating in the Grand Chain which, if the chaperones didn't keep a tight control of decorum, degenerated all too easily into an unseemly romp.

The goldminers' dances were informal affairs. In Greymouth there were two licensed dancehalls in the 1870s, but several of the town's seventy-two pubs offered dancing on the side, with young ladies from across the Tasman ready to help the digger dance the night away—and spend his gold-dust at the bar. A wise girl would take no chances: a Charleston family still possesses a tiny garter-pistol that may have come in handy at anxious moments.

Country people would travel long distances to attend a dance. A group in the far south of Westland rode over a hundred miles through dense forest and along the coast, sidling round rocky bluffs and fording treacherous tidal rivers, to attend the Christmas ball, race meeting and sports at Okarito.

In Canterbury at about the same time they rode to a ball in bullock drays, seated on bags of straw covered with red blankets. As often as not one simply walked, for many miles in some cases, through cold and wet.

In country centres, music could be a problem. In demand at Karamea was a woman who could sing the tunes, and that was all the music; later she graduated to paper-and-comb, and then to the jew's-harp. At Orepuki they had Concertina Harry, such a vigorous player that his instrument was liable to give out after he had played a few dances.

As often as not the only building suitable for a dance would be the local schoolroom. One old sourpuss objected to this in 1880: "Sir, Allow me to draw public attention to the practice that prevails on the part of some of the ruling powers connected with Nelson Creek State School. It is

Music was sometimes a problem where entertainments were planned and groups of amateur musicians were to be found in every community. Circa 1885. (Alexander Turnbull Library)

If there was no other entertainment, isolated country people such as these Marlborough miners would sing together, sometimes with a lone violin or concertina "squeezebox" to accompany them. (Tyree Collection, Nelson Museum)

generally thought that the building was built for educational purposes, apart from that of romping, dancing and other junketings, for which pastimes to be conducted in there are several rooms in the village owned by private persons. It is objected that the schoolhouse should be made use of as a dancing saloon for private amusement." (*Grey River Argus*, 1880.)

In Wellington in the 1880s "Bread-and-Butter" balls were held at the Athenaeum. These were inexpensive affairs where tea, coffee and bread and butter were the only refreshments served. The dancing was so energetic that dust came down from the ceiling and walls and the floor had to be swept during the evening—fortunately there was a tavern right next door where a gentleman could irrigate a dust-tickled throat with more interesting lubricants than tea or coffee.

In 1890 the Wellington Star Boating Club's Ball was held in greater luxury: "Thomas's new buildings had a proper ballroom, the floor was perfect, the decorations included two long racing shells slung across the ceiling, and quaint designs with oars, greenery and flags were hung on the walls. The dais was prettily decorated with ferns and flowers and was furnished like a drawingroom, the Governor and Countess of Onslow sitting up there most of the evening." (*New Zealand Graphic.*)

Dance etiquette was very formal indeed, and under rigid surveillance by the married chaperones, a formidable body who sat up on the dais and kept an eagle eye on the dancers. Every dancer was issued with a programme with a dainty pencil attached, and the first half-hour was devoted by the chaperones or the hostess to introducing the gentlemen to the ladies till everyone's programme was filled.

The Athenaeum Club, Invercargill. Less starchy than their London prototype, New Zealand's Athenaeum Clubs held parties and balls. (Hocken Library)

Manners Street, Wellington, in the 1880s. Despite its lackadaisical appearance in this picture, it was the hub of a gay nightlife. (National Museum)

By 1890, New Zealand was beginning to recover from years of depression and people had more leisure time and more money. Dances were popular and billiards saloons had never had more customers. There was a fine of two pounds if a saloon stayed open after 10 pm. (Alexander Turnbull Library)

It was irregular for a pair of partners to dance more than twice together, but an enterprising young lady might plead fatigue and say "Let's sit this one out, shall we?" to a favoured partner, then they could retire to a discreetly lighted corner of garden or verandah, patrolled only occasionally by some dragonish chaperone.

Refreshments would vary with the occasion. An innocuous claret cup might be the strongest fluid offering, though the host might have a decanter or two in his study for his special cronies; or the fare would be lavish, as at the Masonic Ball in Auckland in 1850: "Choicest viands—turkeys (gelatined and roast) by the dozen—pullets by the score—rounds of beef without end—tongues as tender as they were tranquil and, among numerous other good things, champagne." (*The New Zealander.*)

In the same year, 1850, Canterbury was a much younger settlement than Auckland, but it was determined to celebrate Queen Victoria's birthday with a loyal ball. Charlotte Godley reported: "We were asked for 'dancing at nine' on a magnificent printed card, and found everyone arrived and in superb balldresses, apparently just unpacked from London ... Dancing in three rooms with folding doors between—enclosed verandah for flirtations—but there are only six

The Auckland Militia, called into service in 1863, at the Albert Barracks where Albert Park now stands. Regimental bands were often required to play for dancing at important social functions. (Auckland Public Library)

young ladies, and two of them are old, and the married ladies all dance and, as far as I can judge, don't flirt. The music for this splendid event was provided by two bands, one regimental and one the band of a naval vessel."

For sheer dogged stamina, full marks to Auckland, where in 1879, at an East Tamaki settler's residence: "Proceedings began at 4 pm with croquet, tea at 7, after which the ball opened and continued with only an interval for supper and refreshments, till the sun shone on the dancers. Breakfast was served at 7 am, the music then struck up and the dancers kept it up right through-

out the day till the candles were again in requisition. All night long they danced, then breakfast and a game of croquet closed the ball. Many ladies then started off for home—a ride of fifteen miles, looking just as fresh and rosy as when they began." (*Thames Evening Star*.)

Saturday-night dances must finish sharp at five minutes to midnight lest the Sabbath be fractured. They were therefore called Cinderella dances, for obvious reasons; but there was also an unseemly variant: "Adam and Eve" dances— because "leaves off at twelve". Queen Victoria would not have been amused.

WALKING-OUT AND WEDDINGS

Victorian New Zealanders were strongly influenced by middle-class puritan values and morals inspired by the example of Her Majesty. One of the most intriguing features of this was the mystique of modesty which, for women, meant never revealing their legs and wearing a large number of underclothes yet, for evening social occasions, displaying bare arms and a surprising extent of bosom. Painting the face or powdering the nose was a sure passport to hell-fire. Modesty also meant pretending not to notice that animals were of different sexes—in those days of horse-drawn vehicles they must have had to look the other way very frequently—or that gentlemen sometimes took too much to drink. It was considered ladylike to shriek or faint on receiving bad news, and also to conform to the theory that "a gentleman always knows best about everything".

The brutal realism of back-country life must have seemed a far cry from such ideas, but most women dutifully paid lip-service to them and believed that the most important thing was to be considered *respectable*. It was said a "respectable" woman could travel or walk safely through New Zealand and trust the male strangers with whom she came in contact to be invariably chivalrous and protective—yet one woman who went on a cycling holiday to Rotorua in the 1880s mentions that they were pleased to have her brother in the party, as he could go ahead into the rough little hotels and the crowds of rough men about the railway centres to arrange accommodation and meals.

The Victorian woman of the 1890s' puritan morals revealed neither ankle nor age. This young woman could have been posing for her portrait. As Oscar Wilde wrote: "One should never trust a woman who tells one her real age. A woman who would tell one that would tell one anything." (Hocken Library)

Unless on sporting and social occasions the sexes did not mix freely together. The ladies are here in evidence at the Union Rowing Club, Christchurch, destroyed by fire in 1899. (Canterbury Museum)

The West Coast goldrush increased the population by almost 30,000 in three years. At the christening of the pioneer race, Kaniere, 1866, the miners had plenty to stare at. (Hocken Library)

Goldminers or other groups of labourers would signal to their mates if a female worth staring at appeared on the horizon, and there must have been the overt girl-watchers ready to glimpse a well-turned ankle when the hoops of the crinolines tilted as their wearers mounted the steps of the post office or dismounted from a horse-drawn tram—or, in the later period, from the "safety" bicycle that replaced the "penny-farthing".

Being "talked about" was the most appalling crime, and if a girl was considered "fast" she might as well be dead; one should behave with absolute discretion and never draw attention to oneself. Events such as the coming of the British regiments to New Plymouth during the Land Wars brought this kind of comment (from a letter): "The two girls are a disgrace to everybody belonging to them; since the officers came they are so talked about that there is not a young lady in the place that will associate with them." (Shades of Lydia Bennet in *Pride and Prejudice*.)

In the 1850s and 60s the males far outnumbered the females. As soon as the single women immigrants arrived they were rapidly snapped up as brides, despite the protests of the "gentry" who had brought them out as servants. A leading article in *The Press* urged the Government to bring out many more respectable and useful women suitable for wives: "It is the single men who ever constitute the unsettled roaming element, and where there are no women to marry, men must remain single."

The young swain showed his ardour in those early days by regular visiting, sometimes having to travel long distances on foot. Mrs Grace Hirst wrote breathlessly of her daughter's rather pedestrian courtship: "Mr L. is very regular in his visits—he comes on Friday evenings and on Sunday he mostly comes to tea and goes with us

In a male-dominated society, a girl had to exercise vigilance in the defence of her reputation, but she knew how to dress provocatively.

to church in the evening and then the young people have a walk when they come home we have a glass of milk and bread and butter or cake, he is not at all gentlemanly in his appearance but has the true politeness as far as attending to the comforts and wants of all about him and though *marked* in his attentions there is nothing that even you could find fault with.''

This family had six daughters, and the next young man to arrive in search of a wife was not approved because he was a Dissenter.

Yet another poor suitor wrote to the father saying he was desirous of obtaining a domesticated wife. Papa read the letter to the girls without revealing the name, and they went off into peals of laughter; Isabella borrowed Mamma's checked apron, tucked her sleeves up and danced round the room.

The poet James Barr gave cynical advice on New Zealand courtship:

> *And tell her ye hae got a farm*
> *Laid off in bonnie drills,*
> *And that ye hae a bullock-dray*
> *That gangs on four gude wheels,*
> *And that ye hae baith ducks and hens*
> *That number by the score,*
> *And that ye hae a gross o' pigs*
> *That feed about the door.*
> *But ye mauna speak a word o' love,*
> *They'll only laugh and jeer,*
> *And say, "Gin that be a' ye hae,*
> *Ye needna' hae come here."*
> *Then tell her ye hae lots o' cash,*
> *And that ye'll soon get mair,*
> *And in the course o' twa-three year*
> *Ye'll keep your chaise and pair;*
> *And that she'll never need to wash,*
> *As little bake or brew,*
> *As a' the dirty slaisterin' wark*
> *Will a' be don' by you.*

"Putting up her hair" was the epoch-making moment in a girl's life, when she threw away the black bows of childhood and mastered the difficult art of twisting her hair into the fashionable mode of the day, keeping it there with literally dozens of hairpins.

The *chignon*, more often called a "switch", was no novelty in the 1880s and 1890s. This crucial event had been long prepared for and stitched for. As Evelyn Hosken wrote: "At eighteen we put our hair up and let our skirts right down to the floor; to be really smart one added a slight train, which had to be draped over the arm when walking on the street." This would mean that she had arrived at the age when young

"At eighteen we put our hair up and let our skirts down." A group of the 1890s. (Hocken Library)

gentlemen would be asking her parents' permission to call. Coming-out parties were given for the daughters of the well-to-do, with a special waltz on the programme for the initiates into adult society, giving them a chance to show off their youthful charms to prospective husbands.

As the century wore on and the numbers of maids and men became more even, there was an elaboration in the rituals of courting. We read of gifts of flowers and sweets, and the middle and upper-class custom of chaperoning kept Mother very, very busy. When daughter's young man came to tea, Mother must arrange that the young couple should never be alone together; and when she waved them off to a lecture or a church social, she saw that an older sister or a junior aunt went along to "play gooseberry". This must have led to some amusing scenes, perhaps with our couple walking briskly along the beach, with The Mater or Auntie puffing along a few yards behind, probably not much enjoying herself, but doing her duty as a respectable parent. Whether our sweethearts

If Mamma was not available as chaperone, then Grandmamma was glad to take over. Even the cat is keeping an eye on this couple. (Alexander Turnbull Library)

ever kissed is another interesting question, but answered perhaps by a *Punch* drawing of the 1850s in which a nasty little brother proclaims at the family dinnertable that *he* knows why Sister Emily and Mr Protheroe have both refused helpings of onion sauce.

Chaperonage could be trying; the Christchurch *Globe* said in 1874 that: "There is nothing so tends to shorten the lives of old people, and to injure their health, as the practice of sitting up late, particularly on winter evenings. *This is especially the case when there is a grown-up daughter in the family*. We publish this item at the earnest request of several young men!"

Since young ladies were generally unemployed, except in domestic affairs, every devoted Papa who could afford it would provide his betrothed daughter with a trousseau. She would be expected to contribute some of her own needlework, he would pay for the clothing, household linen and china. (Wanganui Public Museum)

Mr and Mrs Brown might address each other by these names throughout their married life, even within the double brass bed, for which they had paid "twenty-five shillings, complete with mattress". (Canterbury Museum)

Father always calls Mother "Mrs McKee".!!

Popping the question; The dangers of flirtation; How to get married; How to get the money out of Pater for the trousseau (after he has had a well-cooked dinner); and other ingenious advice on How to Capture a Man figure in the *New Zealand Graphic* in the 1890s: "Coral embroidery is a new kind of fancywork, and I saw a bewitching tea-cosy worked in it. Let me suggest that for a bachelor keeping house on his own account one of these dainty and useful cosys would be charming. A girl I knew made one for a young doctor who has just started practice in a pretty little home of his own. He was so struck with the housewifely instinct therein indicated that he at once proposed to her, and the tea-cosy now covers their joint tea-pot."

There was probably a certain amount of pressure brought on girls to marry a man whom the parents thought suitable, but there was one bright young thing in Wellington whose family thought mistakenly they had her safely engaged. Unwisely, her fiancé introduced her to a charming young man who had just arrived off a ship. Alas, the handsome newcomer was entranced with her, she fell in love with him and broke off her engagement, a socially utterly disgraceful act in those days. Often engagements were very long, especially when times were hard and one could just not afford to get married.

Other matters sometimes delayed the walk down the aisle; in 1851 Charlotte Godley writes: "Miss Macfarlane has been on the point of marriage ever since she came, but she cannot make up her mind to be married in book muslin, it must be silk; and another difficulty—that she must wear white satin shoes, therefore she cannot come to church since we have no carriage." On another occasion shipping came in the way of true love: "Jessie Bell is to be married next month— if her trousseau comes in time."

Often the bride would choose a coloured wedding dress which would be suitable as a best dress for the next few years, and it is not until the 1890s that the photographs show white weddings. In the 1880s one young man who had set out on a world tour landed in Wellington after such a rough sea voyage that he vowed he would never set foot on shipboard again; his family in England were concerned that they were not going to see him again, and they arranged for the girl he was engaged to to come out accompanied by her brother, who was "consumptive". By the time they reached Sydney the brother was very ill and, after several months, died. When the poor girl finally arrived in New Zealand she had to have as her wedding dress a mourning dress in delustred

A wedding taxi! The crocheted caps on the horses' ears are perhaps no more absurd than the present-day use of bride dolls. (National Museum)

black silk with deep bands of glistening jet trimming, with a train and small cape. The tale ends more happily, with the couple being married in the church now known as Old Saint Paul's.

Grace Hirst writes dutifully home to her sister in England—punctuation and spelling were not her strong point:

> We were all drest and a hymn sung and had prayers half an hour before the time to start they had a glass of wine then Papa Jane Mary and Annie in the gig with old Dawson, James on Hector and Mr M. the bridegroom on Doctor . . . I had got everything ready and a beautiful luncheon lay ready for them which was ordered by Mr M. and sent up by Black. There were sausage rolls tarts and such a large handsome bridecake and shery wine and decanters on silver stands lent by Mr N. King. They all came in looking so nice and happy and the bridegroom kissed his mother so affectionately it was to me a very touching scene and made me think so much of my own wedding day and Aunt Mary. At three o'clock we sat down to the dinner provided by Black . . . We had what he called stewed

Perhaps it was the late-Victorian insistance upon pre-marital purity that led to the insistance on white weddings. Until late in the century, wedding dresses, while often white, could be of any colour and were generally chosen with practical later use in mind. (Mrs Barbara Richards)

Wedding breakfasts were usually held at home, but this 1890s table looks like an hotel reception. Marbles in the softdrink bottles kept them airtight, but there are wine-bottles on the sideboard. (Alexander Turnbull Library)

beef it was stakes stewed till they were perfectly tender with a beautiful rich brown gravey highly seasoned and garnished with carrots and turnips a roast fillet of veal stuffed boiled fowls tongues and a very nice pastry and for desert almonds and raisins apples and grapes grown and presented by Mr D. Port shery and maidera . . . So now for the dresses, the Bride wore a blue and drab glace silk a white net mantle with three rows of lace and such a pretty bonnet it was blond mixed with pale lilac ribbon and a Marabout feather at one side and orange blossom inside and such a pretty blond veil she had made everything herself but the bonnet and that cost a pound—Mary and Annie wore white straw bonnets trimmed with white ribbon jessamine and white lolly-striped silk dresses and white muslin capes. The Bridegroom wore a black coat cream coloured silk waistcoat with white flowers and lilac trowsers and necktie—Papa black James black coat and trowsers white waistecoat and lilac necktie and all white gloves . . . .

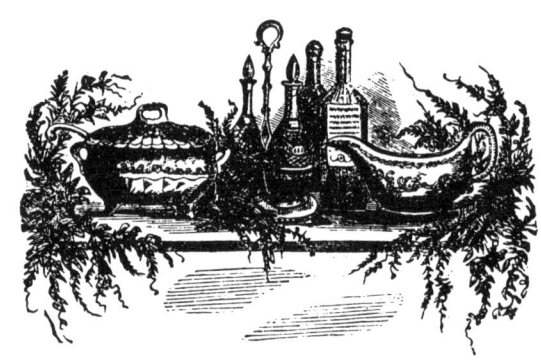

PICNICS, HIGH DAYS AND HOLIDAYS

The beach at St Clair, Dunedin, in the 1880s, with a notable absence of swimmers or suitable seaside clothing. It was a great treat to be allowed to paddle barefoot, although Mamma strictly forbade the removal of hats. A decade later surf bathing was becoming popular. (Hocken Library)

Outings to beach, river or countryside were notable events in the summer life of our greatgrandparents. In the earlier period Saturdays were full working days and Sundays were dedicated to religious observance, picnicking on the Sabbath being considered an ungodly indulgence. Hence picnicking was restricted in the main to public holidays and might be organised by a group of families, or a firm, or by guilds and societies such as the Oddfellows or Rechabites.

Half a dozen people might picnic together, or several hundreds, travelling to the chosen spot on foot, riding on horseback or, latterly, on bicycles, or in horse-drawn vehicles or even by special excursion train.

The picnic meal was the highlight of the day. On arrival the gentlemen would set about building a fireplace while the children scattered to collect firewood, and tea would be brewed up as soon as the kettle was on the boil. Food might be simple sandwiches, cake and fruit, but more sophisticated

For every intrepid rider on the donkey there were twenty envious followers. My Punch is losing no opportunity to advertise his show at the other end of the beach. (Hocken Library)

For the older people Mr Say had provided in a most liberal manner. A tent was erected in one of his paddocks, swings placed in every available branch of his magnificent willow trees, and a free lunch provided which included sucking pig and turkeys. As they disappeared before the attentions of the hungry cricketers and quoit players, fresh relays were brought out."

In Christchurch in the 1880s each group of tradespeople held an annual picnic. When the cabmen relaxed they had races with their horses and running, wives' and children's races, with good prizes donated by business people, including a pair of carriage lamps, deerskin rugs, and meer-schaum pipes. Reporting on the rage for picnics, the *Lyttelton Times* mentions that the mayoral picnic, brewery workers' picnic, bricklayers' picnic and town coroners' picnic are still to be held. (A coroners' picnic sounds rather a grisly affair.) Aucklanders often went no further afield than the Domain; on holidays numbers of small parties could be seen scattered over its glades and copses, and the Good Templars and similar societies would hold their annual festivities there.

hampers might open up to display cold joints and pies, elaborate salads, strawberries and cream and gold-foiled bottles of champagne. If servants were brought along to serve the food and wash up, they would eat their meal at a discreet distance from their masters and mistresses.

Picnic sports and pastimes were much then as they are now, though few parties nowadays would hump along croquet and archery gear as the Victorians so often did. Dress was curiously formal by modern standards, and only towards the end of the century did the children run about barefooted.

The bigger picnics often staged quite elaborate programmes of foot-races and tug-of-wars, with a formal prizegiving and a band to dance to and a barrel or two in the background—ale for the gentlemen, ginger-beer for the ladies and the younger fry.

New Year's Day was a favourite date, and in 1879 the *Thames Star* reported: "The first of January will be remembered as a day of thorough enjoyment for both young and old, if games of all sorts, refreshments at short intervals in the shape of cakes of all varieties, syrups and ginger beer ad libitum for the young can make you glad.

Organised games were often played at larger picnics and "Farmer in the Dell" was a favourite with the younger generation.

Special excursions by train or tram attracted an enthusiastic following. Even Grandpa in the bowler is off for a day's fun at the beach. (Hocken Library)

The picnic luncheon was the highlight of the day, particularly if it was Christmas Day, although the Victorians found it difficult to adjust to a midsummer Christmas, and the "home" custom of hot roasted meat, with plum pudding to follow, persisted. (Canterbury Museum)

Sometimes there were adventures. When a party of young ladies went to a gorge near Geraldine for a picnic in a large double-seated buggy, they allowed their horse to wander and could not find it in the evening. After hunting hill and dale without success they put one of their number who was unable to walk in the buggy, and the remainder took up the shafts and set out for town. At one stage a swollen creek blocked the way, but the ladies, undaunted, waded through, hauling the buggy after them in water up to the waist.

Jane Maria Richmond tells of a picnic in Taranaki: "The day was the loveliest imaginable— a party of young male pedestrians started early, and about eight o'clock two bullock carts set out with the elders and the youngsters. Riding in these carts is a fine healthy exercise no doubt. Who can describe the crossing of a river? Every joint seems dislocated, every portion bruised."

Picnic at Lowry Bay, Wellington, 1891. The sailor's uniforms look rather un-British. Perhaps the men were from a visiting foreign warship? (Halse Collection, Alexander Turnbull Library)

In those days good-weather travel on harbour or lake was more comfortable than over the wretched roads—Nelson folk in 1866 sailed to Motueka on the steamer *Wallaby*, spent the day rambling and riding and came back by moonlight on a rippling sea. And there were similar trips elsewhere: "Parliamentary Rates—*City of Cork*—will run excursion parties from Auckland to Riverhead and back at single fare of 3s each, or one penny a mile, on Saturdays only, leaving at 12.30 and returning about 5 pm." (*Evening Star*, 1877.)

School fêtes and gardenparties were special occasions, and dressing up for the Grand Parade was exciting for the children but hard work for the parents, who had risen early in the morning to thread daisy chains or make paper flowers. (Dunedin, 1900)

In Wellington the weather often upset the best laid plans: "Miss Holmes has been getting up a large moonlight boating picnic, but as I write it is pouring with rain and bitterly cold, so I suppose it will have to be put off until some fine night." (*New Zealand Graphic*, 1891.)

The Queen's birthday was always celebrated most loyally, and in Dunedin in 1860 there was a harbour excursion, boat races, and a concert which, the press reported, was for charitable purposes—and that there was a need for a great deal of charity on the part of the audience. Wellington in 1890 staged a ball at Government House for High Society and an electric-light display at the Basin Reserve for the lesser beings. The same year in Auckland the Volunteers staged a mock battle at the North Shore, the highlight being when two ladies set off two submarine mines which sent up a geyser-like spray of water. The socialites then dispersed to a festive luncheon, and the troops and public to the Takapuna Races.

There was always a wag or two to provide the laughs. An exchange of hats, a pipe and a cigarette out of place, and the pretence at beer drinking invited a giggle. Circa 1897. (Alexander Turnbull Library)

Even the miners around Greymouth downed tools for Christmas in 1866: "Although everyone is so intent on the race for wealth, we are to indulge in races of another kind during Christmas week. A sports committee has been appointed, and a sufficient sum of money has been sub-scribed by the inhabitants to provide a series of amusements. On Tuesday we are to have a regatta, to be followed the next day by athletic sports." In Kumara in 1882 the people went in for novelty races at their Christmas sports; there was a 100-yards race for barmaids, of whom five or six lined up for the start. A Miss Jacobs proved the winner, and was happily rewarded with a trimmed hat; the second prize was also a hat and the third a pair of stays.

Avondale Racing Club's Spring Meeting, 1898. Horseracing attracted more people than any other outdoor entertainment. The first anniversary of settlement in New Zealand was celebrated in 1841 by racing horses on the beach. (Auckland Public Library)

No picnic was complete without a stone jar of gingerbeer, and sometimes a bottle or two of the real thing. The small boy on the box seat is neglecting his duties as a chaperone. (Tesla Collection, Alexander Turnbull Library)

From Thames comes a report of how that town saw the old year out in 1879: "The old custom of welcoming in the New Year passed very tamely here. At the hour when churchyards are supposed to yawn, however, there were a good number of people in Brown and Albert Streets, when an open air concert commenced—and subsequently a large party paraded the town, filling the early morning air with stentorian melody." Mr Whitson's paddock near his brewery was the venue for the New Year sports in Auckland, which was a Scottish occasion, with the usual putting the stone, tossing the caber, tilting, Highland dancing, quoits, and bagpipe playing.

The anniversary day of the first landing in each province immediately became an important date for celebration, especially for those who had been companions on the long and arduous journeys in

Te Aroha and the Waihou (Thames) River, with a tourist coach on the barge, which was powered by the river current. Second only to Rotorua in popularity were the hot springs at Te Aroha, where a 10s ticket entitled the bearer to twenty-five public or fifteen private baths. (National Museum)

those little ships. In 1850 Wellington held an anniversary fête on Te Aro Flat which offered aquatic sports, horse races, and "rural sports" which included greasy pole, soap-necked geese, grinning through horse collars, a donkey race, a bull race, a war dance, a "native female" race, smoking and drinking matches, and a rolls-and-molasses match. A firework display rounded off the festivities.

Our Victorians certainly knew how to enjoy themselves in the open air—so long as the sanctity of Sunday observance was not interfered with: "Firing of guns during Divine Service on the Sabbath—It was Prince Albert's birthday but the timing offended hundreds by the unbecoming interruption." (*The New Zealander*, 1850.)

✪✪✪✪ TRAVEL AND TOURISM ✪✪✪✪

As the many scenic attractions of New Zealand were first discovered and reported, sketched and photographed, people set off on expeditions to see them for themselves and came back to spread the story of their experiences.

Though the hotelkeepers and coaching agents did their best to make travel easy and comfortable, it was often highly uncomfortable by twentieth-century standards and not infrequently dangerous. The roads were appallingly rough or could become quagmires of mud in wet weather. Coaches were unheated, and able-bodied passengers were expected to walk up the steeper gradients so that the horses could struggle to the summit; rivers could flood, and passengers and horses could be swept away and drowned, or might have to wait, shivering and half-starving, for the waters to subside.

The steep road over Arthur's Pass to Otira could terrify the weak-nerved. One gentleman incurred the contempt of his male fellow-passengers: he was so terrified of the precipitous descent that he insisted that his wife, who had a seat inside the Cobb coach, should take his seat "up top" so that he could sit inside and say his prayers till they reached their destination.

Boat trips on sea or lake could be fatally hazardous, and even if the traveller reached his hotel or accommodation house in safety he might find poor food, a damp or dirty bed, and a torment of fleas or other pests.

A typical traveller of the 1850s, the intrepid Kate Hadfield, set off with her husband, the Rev. Octavius, to make the journey from Auckland to Wanganui overland, because no ships were available. They were accompanied by some Maori

Brighton House, to which families of holidaymakers came from Dunedin, twelve miles distant, to bathe in the sharp clear water of the South Pacific Ocean. (Hocken Library)

The Wanganui River was navigable for 140 miles, and a regular weekly steamer service between Wanganui and Pipiriki was begun in 1892. From Pipiriki, lighter craft were used for day trips to the river's upper reaches, where there were rapids, magnificent bush and high cliffs, and Maori villages.

guides, and had a tent specially made for the trip. "At two o'clock Mr Morgan called us. I had just got to sleep being tormented with mosquitos and did not feel at all inclined to move. However, as none of us had taken our clothes off, it did not take long to get up. Mr Eyre had a large fire burning and we had breakfast, and sat in the chimney to have prayers." The party set off again by canoe, following a creek and then the Waikato River. "At twelve o'clock we went ashore to dinner and while they were getting dinner I gave baby a bath in the river and put him into some clean clothes. He seemed to enjoy it very much, dear little fellow, he gives no trouble at all."

It was midsummer, and the weather was terribly hot: "After dinner we soon got out of the wood and came to what we thought was flat country, but to our disappointment we found that every quarter of a mile we had to go down and then up again very steep places about twenty times which quite tired our patience."

She continues with a description of the bush-clad gorges of the Wanganui: "It is worth coming to see and I had heard so much about the rapids. I thought it would be like coming down a waterfall. When Mrs Kissling was trying to frighten me she said it was very unlike anything I had ever seen, but it was only like going over a rough sea for a few yards."

Later this river became very popular with overseas and local tourists, the voyage often being made by paddle steamer. The magnificent bush, glimpses of Maori village life and the excitement

of negotiating the numerous rapids made a good holiday, with accommodation provided at the hotel at Pipiriki. The large stern-wheeler *Manuwai*, which could carry 400 passengers, was mainly used for day excursions in the lower tidal reaches. One man remembers " . . . with her stern thrashing, and her decks swarming with picnic parties in colourful holiday dress, she made an unforgettable picture". Her usual destination was Hipango Park, where the fireman would

The Wanganui River terminus was Pipiriki. When the picture was taken, in the 1880s, it was a typical Maori village of the period. (Alexander Turnbull Library)

When gold fever brought men to the Shotover River, Queenstown was born. It became a borough in 1866. For many years the lake steamers carried goods, residents and tourists across the lake to the sheep stations, and up to the valleys that led into the mountains. (Hocken Library)

dispense boiling water from the ship's boiler to tea-making picnickers.

Coastal shipping played an important part in the transport of sightseers from one wonder of New Zealand to another, and by 1879 the Union Steamship Company's early paddle-steamer fleet had grown to a number of ships which formed a "steam girdle" round the two islands and plied a service to Australia as well.

As early as 1879 this company had commissioned the wellknown writer and poet, Thomas Bracken, to produce a guidebook entitled *The New Zealand Tourist*. In the introduction to this book he tells us: "In this age of cheap expeditions, when a voyage round the world is looked upon as an undertaking of less magnitude than a journey of a few hundred miles would have appeared to our fathers, books of the class of this compilation are in general demand."

Bracken disembarked his traveller at Bluff and showed him the sights of Invercargill, then sent him off by rail to Kingston, with a side trip to Te Anau and Manapouri if required. The fast express train from Gore to Kingston affectionately known as the *Kingston Flyer* was pulled by a tough little Yankee "K" locomotive and carried the tourist on to board the steamer for a sail up Lake Wakatipu and a view of its beautiful mountain scenery. Queenstown had several comfortable hotels by this time.

Most travellers would make a journey to the head of the lake, perhaps staying at Bryant's

Hotel, the boat pulling in for picnics on the way: "The ladies laid the cloth, the hampers were unpacked, and we were all speedily engaged in discussing the merits of host Eichardt's cold fowls and lamb, the relish of the latter heightened by mint sauce. Tea for some, and malt and sherry for others wound up our repast, and we envied none living. Our hunger satisfied, the sketchers scattered, each selecting his favourite point of view."

There was so much to see, including the Arrow diggings and the Macetown reefs (the latter would have been a walk or horseback journey, with many fordings of the river). The people of Arrowtown found that as well as being a mining and farming centre, their little town was becoming a tourist attraction, and in 1882 the *Lake County Press* gently admonished the citizens: "It seems that this district is yearly increasing in favour with tourists and other visitors. It should therefore be a point of honour to respect them; not always to stare at them, and wonder who they are. Anyone may, with a respectful manner, afford them that information they so much desire."

Mount Cook in the very earliest days was visited by riding parties who carried their own food and equipment and camped in the valley near the site of the old Hermitage. Bracken's *Guide* told travellers that if they wished to journey back to Timaru they would have to find their own way by horse, and advised them that they could depend on the hospitality of the station-holders for accommodation.

A coach with three intrepid lady tourists fords a creek on the way to Mount Cook. Parasols shield them from the sun, their luggage is securely covered from dust or rain. (Ross Collection, Alexander Turnbull Library)

The White Terrace. On 10 June 1886, Mount Tarawera erupted violently, destroying a village, with considerable loss of life, and drowning the famous Pink and White silica terraces beneath the new level of Lake Rotomahana. (National Museum)

By 1887 tourists took the train to Fairlie, slept the night there, and left the following morning by coach for Lake Pukaki, travelling over an unformed road. During the next bumpy day at least fourteen mountain torrents had to be crossed, and many smaller streams, before the Hermitage was reached by nightfall. One can only hope that the blessed mountain deigned to unveil herself to their deserving eyes. The safe arrival of the coach was reported by the despatch of a carrier pigeon to the Pukaki Hotel.

Tourists landed at the busy port of Napier from other parts of New Zealand and overseas to make the overland journey to Taupo and the hot lakes. Once, as the passengers boarded the coach for the journey inland, an English visitor discovered there was not a seat left for him. As there were several Maoris sitting "up-top" he stood back expecting one of them to offer or be ordered to give up his seat for his "better". The "pukka sahib" slowly realised that in this colony one man's money was as good as another's, whether he was white or brown, poor or rich.

To sink into a hot sulphur bath at one of the hotels at Ohinemutu must have been a joy to the bone-weary travellers after the rugged and winding journey from the coast. After a good meal guests could stroll or sit in the attractive gardens, or visit a Maori whare and meetinghouse and glimpse the Maori way of life which, in the nineteenth century, was markedly different from the Pakeha's.

The famous but ill-fated Pink and White Terraces in this area caused a rolling-stone correspondent of the *New Zealand Herald* in 1883 to become lyrical: "I have seen the Himalayas, the Blue Mountains of Tartary, Fujiyama of Japan, the Rocky Mountains and the Sierra Nevadas, but for delicate, unique beauty, for chaste design and sublime detail of construction, never have I gazed upon so wonderful a sight as the White Terrace. When we had feasted our eyes upon its exquisite beauties the ladies in our party filed slowly away, as if spellbound, while we (the sterner sex) divested ourselves of our outward garb of civilisation." The males then enjoy a swim: "But in place of fairies,

The firm of Cobb & Co., which operated coaches in Australia, never did operate them in New Zealand. Coaches of the type they used were brought into this country and were known as "Cobb" coaches. Sometimes they were operated under licence, using the name of Cobb & Co. This scene is at New Plymouth, 1871.

Waiwera Hotel, thirty miles north of Auckland. Robert Graham, who was Superintendent of Auckland 1862-65, could be called the founder of the tourist industry. He leased land at Waiwera and developed the area for visitors to the hot springs. (Hocken Library)

the mermaids and all the nymphs, there were one or two dark sirens around, whose well-turned forms stood out like bronze statues against the white silica rock as they looked on with lustrous eyes and smoked short pipes, which filled the ambient air with the fumes of strong tobacco. When we had enjoyed the luxuries of the bath we found the guide Sophia and the ladies waiting for us impatiently under a clump of tea-tree." Three years later these lovely terraces were to be destroyed for ever by the eruption of Mt Tarawera, which caused the loss of many lives.

Many photographs remain of the old coaches laden with warmly wrapped passengers, some perched precariously on roof seats and looking very vulnerable if the horses should shy or a wheel break. There must have been several hundreds of tourist vehicles operating in the last century, from the beautifully painted and upholstered Cobb & Co coaches, which had special springing for the colonial non-roads, to smaller coaches with roll-down tarpaulin sides and roofs, to scantily-protected wagonettes. The advantage to the traveller was that the companies had a network of regular services over most of the country, and journeys could be planned in advance. Usually the vehicles departed from an hotel, where patrons would have had a meal to set them up for a few hours until the first change of horses and the re-victualling of humans. "Aicken's" on the West Coast near Otira was a roadhouse in the coaching days, and the noonday halt at its diningroom was hungrily anticipated by travellers who relished Mrs Aicken's celebrated cookery.

The Diningroom, Wairakei. (Hocken Library)

62

The head of Lake Te Anau, and the beginning of the Milford Track, 1895. Behind the elegant lady-tramper a photographer—one of the Burton brothers?—is taking out his camera. (National Museum)

Summer excursions by steamer (below is the SS Tarawera) were run from Dunedin to Milford Sound. In 1888 Mackinnon's Pass was discovered and the Milford Track was born. Until 1940 the Track was the only land route to Milford. (Hocken Library)

One lady who found the organised gaiety rather a bore wrote her thoughts on first sighting Milford: "Truly, the boundless liberty of communion with Nature in her vaster temples fills us with a sense of space, and of a large symmetry that outdoes the imagination. And yet, though imagination cannot reach her limits, never is this sense so abiding in us as when, weary of the elusive quality of the world's interests, we turn to the Earth-mother and receive her ample reward."

"The Finest Walk in the World" was opened to tourists in 1890, and the first woman to tramp over it was Mrs Samuel Moreton, the painter's wife, who recorded in the visitor's book: " . . . delighted with my trip as I am the first lady to have crossed from Te Anau to Milford". The Pompolona Hut on the Milford Track originally consisted of a large sleeping tent, a diningroom under a large calico fly with an equally flimsy kitchen, none of which would have given much protection when the Fiordland rain descended.

Numerous small hotels, a coaching-day apart, thrived all over the country, and there are enough of them still standing to enable us to picture them in their prosperous "red plush" era. Mrs Wilson gave notes on the décor of the parlour of the little inn at Arrowtown: "Acres of woolwork covered the furniture, beaded mats of grotesque design bestrewed the tables; upon the walls hung many coloured prints in fir-cone frames; and on the mantelshelf, evidently the *pièce de résistance* (O, spirit of Oscar Wilde) stood a high vase, full of miraculous wax flowers, under a glass shade!"

The splendours of Milford Sound would have been broadcast by the passengers on the many ships that called there, often those on the Dunedin to Melbourne service. An excursion to Milford by steamer in the 1890s organised diversions for the tourist—concerts, dances, tableaux, fireworks.

Foxton in the 1870s, terminus of one of the earliest railway lines in the North Island. With wooden rails and a horsedrawn carriage, it ran from The Square in Palmerston North to the port of Foxton, where goods and passengers were embarked for New Plymouth and Nelson. (Alexander Turnbull Library)

63

By 1887, when this photograph was taken near Napier, travel by railway had become familiar. The occasion was a trial run for a brand-new locomotive. (New Zealand Railways)

About this time Mrs Elizabeth Sutherland opened an accommodation house at the Sound, and she and her husband Donald became part of the legend of Milford.

Travel became far more smooth and comfortable as our country moved into the railway age, and to take a journey now meant farewells on the platform, with all the drama of guards, flags, signalboxes and colourful engines hissing and thundering. The engines had personalities of their own and names such as *The Snake*, *Ada*, and *Josephine*; *Meg Merrilies*, *Ivanhoe*, *Rob Roy* and

On 12 December, 1893, the line between Greymouth and Hokitika was opened, and a special excursion train marked the occasion. The fashionable young woman in the feather boa is Mrs Seddon, wife of the prime minister familiarly known as "King Dick". (New Zealand Railways)

Jeannie Deans were named after Sir Walter Scott's characters.

The early railway coaches were small, with varnished wooden seats and furnished with wax-match-strikers and brass spittoons at strategic intervals. There were ornate wrought-iron luggage racks, perhaps an embossed metal ceiling, and oil lamps for lighting. It is amusing to hear that one paterfamilias, who held a high office in the Government, always travelled in stately solitude in a first-class carriage, while his wife managed their numerous brood in the second class.

Christchurch railway staff, with a top-hatted stationmaster and his uniformed staff. Can Napoleon be serious? (Canterbury Museum)

Often the train journey led to a pleasurable holiday at the seaside or country with a stay at one of the large, rambling wooden boardinghouses which have been a feature of our country from the 1870s to the present-day era of motels. Good company, fishing, wagonette trips, long days on the sands and in the seas were enjoyed by people from the towns and from up country. Usually there was abundant home-grown home-cooked food, with plenty of cream, fresh-caught fish or whatever food was special to the district. This kind of holiday must have been especially appreciated by weary mothers.

A typical invitation to sample boardinghouse hospitality in this Palmerston North advertisement of 1883: "Notice of Removal—Mr Dawick, Boarding House and Residence, late of Main St., begs to

NOTIFY the Public that his NEW BUILDING in Rangitikei St. is now completed—Travellers will find every convenience and comfort, coupled with attention and civility—BATHROOMS, well-ventilated BEDROOMS, SITTING-ROOMS, PARLOUR—the TABLE being WELL-KNOWN needs no recommendation.''

The coming of better transport enabled families to build their own primitive baches or cribs at the seaside and along the riverbanks—fine fun for fathers and children but perhaps not so popular with Mamma, who might prefer a farmhouse holiday. Many farmers' wives took in city families as summer boarders—a welcome addition to the farmer's wife's housekeeping funds, and a valuable social link between Town and Country.

As the early settlers prospered some of them were able to afford a trip "Home", and the advent of steam was making sea travel really comfortable and fast, although in 1877 you could still book a passage on an A1 clipper sailing ship such as the *May Queen* for a voyage from Auckland to London. In the mid 1880s the steamships took about forty days to reach Britain and the fares ranged from saloon, at sixty guineas and upwards, to second, forty guineas, and steerage eighteen guineas. One observer commented on New Zealanders: " . . . everybody travels. A roadman who has been employed by the government for the last ten years is in England for a spell, just to look around. Even labourers think nothing of a voyage from Canterbury to Auckland to see a friend."

Six miles by ferry from Auckland, Takapuna Beach in 1898, with holidaymakers enjoying sun, sand, and horseback riding. Victorian modesty still prevented many from the enjoyment of surf bathing. (Auckland Public Library)

A trip "Home". This Wellington lady is about to make the pilgrimage, complete with portmanteaux, wicker baskets and deck chair. "Home" was never far from the minds of the settlers, but often a generation or two passed before money and opportunity became available.

Bedford House, Dunedin. "Private Boarding Establishment for Families and Gentlemen." Solo ladies, apparently, had to find accommodation elsewhere. (Hocken Library)

Walking was one of the few permitted activities on Sundays and the beach naturally attracted many. This is Cave Rock, Sumner. At the other end of the beach were the donkeys and the bathing-machines—probably forbidden pleasures on the Sabbath. (Canterbury Museum)

 # THE GREAT OUTDOORS

Travelling on foot, or on Shanks's pony as they called it, was often a necessity right through the Victorian era. Horses first, and later bicycles, were sometimes an alternative, and public transport developed as the century drew towards its close. But a lot more walking was done then than it is now, and as much for enjoyment as for simply taking oneself from point A to point B.

Active mountaineering was popular and not unladylike, and even the tougher climbs such as Mt Egmont appealed to both sexes. Jane Maria Atkinson had the distinction of being the first woman to climb this mountain with some members of her family, and she had wisely made herself some canvas dungarees for the trip. In those days aged Maoris were often seen sitting alone above the bushline, communing with the spirits of the tribal past. Elsewhere around the country energetic climbers posed for their photographs on top of Ben Lomond, Mt Cargill and

Mt Tongaririo. By the 1890s thriving field, rambling, tramping and mountaineering clubs were available for those with these interests.

For some the exhilaration of a day's riding with gallops along a beach or over pastures, or a cross-country trek, was the ideal exercise. Ladies must wear riding habits, and sidesaddle was *de rigueur*. In the country parties of friends would assemble and ride the many miles from one sheep station to another, staying a day or two at each for tennis or cricket and music and dancing. Competitive horsemanship was encouraged by the events at the A & P shows, and around the country there were hunt clubs—in 1893 the *Poverty Bay Herald* reported enthusiastically if a trifle inaccurately: "The county drain proved a stopper for many, including one dapper gentleman on a little grey, both landing in it and emerging covered with a rich alluvial deposit. The day's run finished at Mr Arthur's house (The Willows), where 'Tally

This photograph was taken at Dawson Falls House, Mt Egmont, and there must be many family albums which hold similar pictures. In 1855, Jane Maria Atkinson was the first woman to climb to the mountain's top. (Alexander Turnbull Library)

Ho' was sounded and the members were entertained. Five women and twenty men rode to the hunt."

Quite early in our history we read of polo matches and gymkhanas, probably introduced by military men retired from India. Gymkhana events might include novelty races such as one where each rider had to light a cigar and unfurl a Japanese parasol before starting.

Horses were the universal means of transport and ladies rode sidesaddle, not for elegance, but because they "could maintain better balance and greater control of the animal"—a claim not likely to be upheld today. The stylish rider is Miss Brown, competing at an undated Riverton show.

Of the garden pastimes, croquet held pride of place for many years before giving way to lawn tennis, for this sedentary game required no more than ordinary outdoor clothing, elderly players should show their juniors a thing or two, and there was time for leisurely scandal and flirtation—the latter, particularly, if Miss Lydia bashed Mr Reginald's ball into the shrubbery and they had to go off together to retrieve it.

In this 1895 photograph Guide Clark leads a party of amateur mountaineers over to a glacier in the Mt Cook area. (Canterbury Museum)

Undoubtedly the real national sport was horse-racing, whether at little neighbourhood meetings or at metropolitan race weeks where the ladies donned all their very latest frills and furbelows for strolling on the lawns to the music of brass bands and the sound of discreet social gossip. There were garden parties, dances, and a ball at the Provincial Chambers in Christchurch, while informal race-meetings like those held on the Porirua shoreline in 1862 would attract amateur riders from all around, with a wide variety of steeds. Five hundred people turned out on this particular occasion, which concluded with a gay ball at Lloyd's Travellers' Rest in the evening.

A luncheon party at the Avondale Racecourse, 1899. (Auckland Public Library)

Belltopper hats for men, crinolines with white gloves and bonnets, were normal attire for enjoying archery. It was a sport which attracted more women than men until 1880, when it lost popularity altogether. This photograph was taken at some time during the 1870s, in Hagley Park, Christchurch. (Canterbury Museum)

Tennis, at first, was almost as peaceful. It was permissible for a gentleman to play in his shirt-sleeves, and the underarm pat-ball service and the slow tempo of the early game allowed it to be played by ladies in long skirts and down-to-the-wrist leg-of-mutton sleeves. But in the 1890s clubs were formed in town and country and tennis had become a serious game instead of a gentle social pastime, though young and frivolous members went to the club in search of a match of more than one kind.

Archery made its appearance in Auckland in 1872 and flourished until displaced by tennis. It demanded an open range of up to 100 yards, and as few of even the most spacious and gracious Victorian gardens could offer this, public areas such as the Christchurch Botanical Gardens provided "archery lawns". Here a Governor, Lord Normanby, competed in 1878—presumably with the regulation three dozen arrows at sixty and eighty yards. The ladies' ranges were fifty and sixty yards.

For the Victorian social equivalent of what is today called the "jet set", cycling had an irresistible appeal. The first penny-farthing bicycles that came into the country provided great fun for spectators as the male riders wobbled and swerved about, struggling to keep their balance on the rough roads. Some found tricycles were safer, and more genteel, and the *Tricyclist's Indispensable Handbook* was a bestseller in the bookshops. But it was the "safety bicycle", mass-produced and imported in the 1880s, which caused a transport revolution and, for the young especially, brought a greater mobility and means of getting out of

range of restricting authority—hence a young lady who took up cycling ran the risk of being called "fast", and her parents were censured accordingly.

Men were interested in long-distance rides, and in racing, and so bicycling clubs sprang into being: "To Amateur Bicyclists—All Gentlemen interested in the formation of a Bicycle Club in Christchurch are requested to meet at the Commercial Hotel." (*Lyttelton Times*, 1879). As a result of this meeting the Pioneer Bicycle Club was formed. Several years later this city had the Atalanta Ladies' Cycling Club, with Miss Blanche Lough as captain

Early cycling clubs wore very fancy and not always very practical club uniforms. (Canterbury Museum)

68

Dunedin Football Club—an early First XV. A touring team from Auckland Provincial Clubs played a combined Dunedin team in the first interprovincial match on 22 September, 1875. (Hocken Library)

Cricket has always been popular as a summer game. It is said that as early as 1834 Henry Williams ordered cricket gear to be sent from England. Early clubs were often social groups formed by the employees of a company, and this is the Washco Cricket Team, Palmerston North, in 1900, the scorer absorbed in mental arithmetic. (Palmerston North Public Library)

The Devonport Bowling Club, 1896. Little sign of modern uniform-mania for bowls devotees, but they probably had just as much fun. (Auckland Public Library)

and Mrs Burn as secretary, but the proposed uniform of the club touched off a spate of letters to the editor:

> Sir, A ladies' cycling club having been formed, "Aroaleat" suggests that a uniform hat and tunic be decided upon, and follows with some very vague remarks about "rational" dress. Now as a few lady cyclists have appeared in knickerbockers, and as a skirt is not mentioned, I conclude this is the dress referred to. I have taken the trouble to call on the greater part of the ladies who entertain the idea of joining the club, and they are decided upon one thing—that if the club uniform is to include the "rational" garment referred to, they refuse to appear in public in such a "get up". "A's" remarks about a girl having to don one of her little brother's suits to ride in are not any more rational than the idea suggested by the writer. The bicycle makers here have supplied several ladies with machines adapted to their dress, and I think the ladies are very well content with the present arrangements, and a good majority are determined to resist adopting any uniform that a lady would hesitate to wear. Yours etc.—Uniform. (*The Press*, 1892.)

Pity the poor caddy! Dunedin, naturally, built New Zealand's first golf course in 1870. (Canterbury Museum)

Footballs and cricket bats seem to have come ashore in the very earliest immigrants' luggage. Bowls made their début in Auckland in 1860. Lacrosse had a brief vogue in the 1870s and 1880s but gave way to hockey.

Rod and gun and their devotees were to have a more profound effect in the country itself. A Frenchman once observed that no Englishman could be happy unless he killed something every day before lunch, and upper-class immigrants were shocked to find the new country so uncannily empty of gamebirds, fish, and game animals— wild pig and the native pigeon were about all the sport offering.

So acclimatisation societies sprang up in the 1860s and 70s, and in 1866 the *Nelson Examiner* was announcing: "For Sale: Superior single-

70

This shooting party holds an interesting assortment of firearms, from .22 rifle to .44 Winchester, and shotguns. The photograph was taken on Kapiti Island before 1900, when the island was declared a reserve. (Alexander Turnbull Library)

An artist's idea of New Zealand pheasant shooting, 1900. The sportsman (?) is shooting at murderously short range. (Auckland Weekly News)

barrelled guns and superior double-barrelled guns—also Hall & Sons superior glass gunpowder; Patent shot, all sizes, Eley's best waterproof caps and gun wads—at H. Hounsell's Store, near new Post Office."

A sportsman might have a dull day. "Went out shooting for the day—only shot two quail, a lark and a mocker," records a diary of 1887. But four members of the Canterbury Rabbit Club, with the Governor as their guest, bagged sixty-one rabbits in a three-hour drive in the late 1870s.

The dangers of fording swift rivers were unfamiliar to newcomers from Britain and drownings became so common as to earn the name of "the New Zealand death". The ability to swim could make the difference between life and death, and it is not surprising that public swimming baths and clubs were soon established in towns of any size.

"The Lyttelton Bathing Shed—On Monday a female nearly lost her life while bathing, and was only rescued by the merest chance by a man passing at the moment . . . The female attendant at the baths offered no assistance, there was no boat, no lifebuoy, and not so much as a rope within reach." (*The Press*, 1865.)

Custom declared that the sexes should not mix

It was not until 1912 that women were allowed to compete in national swimming events. This Wanganui school race is probably pre-1912, but may be Edwardian rather than Victorian. (Wanganui Public Museum)

for bathing. The males took to the water clad in assorted garments from nothing at all through to stockinette tops and below-the-knee trousers with striped bands. Many of our long beaches would have been almost empty in the early days, and the ladies would choose a secluded bathing place further along the beach. Probably very few of them could swim. One person has childhood memories of watching a portly woman going bathing in a voluminous blue serge bathing costume with frills and white braid right down to her calves with bloomers, stockings, and beach shoes which laced up above the ankles; when she was in the water the costume floated up all round her. Swimming would have been difficult if not impossible in such a costume.

THE ENTERTAINERS

The handwritten caption by T.M. Hocken reads: "Class distinction prevailed in the early days. A selection was made of guests for a trip down the harbour. Mr Greer was manager of the new steamboat service to Port Chalmers—circa 1861." (Hocken Library)

Turgid melodrama and broad farce were New Zealand's dramatic favourites all through the Queen's long reign, with Shakespeare and Sheridan the perennial runners-up. Touring companies' producers showed an extraordinary ingenuity in representing such disasters as fires and shipwrecks on stage, and even horseraces.

The theatres themselves were lavishly decorated and lighted, as were the music halls, with boxes for the wealthy and bars for the thirsty. Enterprising publicans soon added theatrettes to their premises to attract trade and in 1850 we find the Britannia Saloon in Auckland advertising the attractions of "Mr Anderson, the Celebrated Wizard and Ventriloquist—Box 3s, Pit 2s, Gallery 1s—No Smoking."

The titles of the plays conjure up visions of the plots: *The Road to Ruin, All That Glitters Is Not Gold, The Irish Detective, Famine, The Wages of Sin, Snared, Muldoon's Picnic, The Ticket-of-Leave Man.* Usually the newspapers' dramatic critics gave a full synopsis of the plays so that theatregoers knew beforehand what they were letting themselves in for.

Melodrama should so churn the emotions that it was politic to follow them up with a one-act farce or burlesque. A typical Auckland programme of 1864 at the Prince of Wales Theatre: "Last evening the drama of *The Sailor of France* was followed by the burlesque of *Villikins and his Dinah.* There was a capital audience, and the burlesque seems to be an attraction to the gods."

Theatres and music halls quickly sprang up, but a great deal of the entertainment was homemade. On the right of this amateur theatrical group is Alfred Domett, poet and Premier (1863). The play was She Stoops to Conquer, *circa 1870. (Alexander Turnbull Library)*

These posters on the corner of Cathedral Square and Worcester Street, Christchurch 1865, advertise the versatility of Christy's Minstrels, who promise nightly entertainment ranging from burlesque and opera to the Swiss Sisters *and* Lucrezia Borgia*! (Canterbury Museum)*

From the booming 1860s onwards New Zealand attracted leading artists from all over the world—names now almost forgotten, but they were the great stars of their day: Charles Dillon, Dion Boucicault, J.L. Toole with Irene Vanbrugh, Janet Achurch, and the famous American comedian Joe Jefferson whose Dunedin son-in-law, Benjamin Farjeon, wrote plays that had successful runs in London as well as New Zealand.

Other celebrated overseas entertainers included the notorious Irish adventuress Lola Montez, scandal-star of Melbourne—Madame Cora "World-Famous Hypnotiste", Carl Hertz "Premier Prestidigitateur and Illusionist", The Fakir of Oolu and "his beautiful Entranced Lady", and the famous midgets, General Tom Thumb and his wife, favourites of the great Duke of Wellington. Regular and popular entertainers were the Inimitable Charles Thatcher and his wife Madame Vitelli; Thatcher it was who first coined our familiar phrase "old identities" in a satirical ballad about the over-conservative Dunedinites.

For the last three decades of the century the Williams & Musgrove opera company of Melbourne would send over a large cast every autumn, often with a Gilbert and Sullivan programme, with a long itinerary culminating in Auckland in Race Week. "The Opera Company have had a great success at Thames during their season of six nights, the theatre not being large enough to hold all who desired to be present," wrote *The Globe* of Christchurch in 1874.

The country being without benefit of cinema or television, the papers focussed public attention on live entertainment and theatrical gossip reached almost Hollywood proportions: "Mr Kyrle Bellew's reputation as a lady-killer has preceded him to America, and during his stay there it is announced that fathers, brothers and sweethearts will patrol the neighbourhood of Wallack's Theatre with shotguns on their shoulders." (*Otago Daily Times*, 1885.)

Vaudeville flourished from the 1870s onwards and in the 1890s John Fuller of Dunedin and his sons founded an enterprise that made "Fullers" a household word throughout the Dominion right until the advent of the talking films that swept the dainty soubrettes, the bawdy comics, the jugglers, the ventriloquists, the acrobats, the adagio dancers, and the musical-glasses virtuosi into a regrettable oblivion.

The rash of big new theatres in the 1870s was a phenomenon of the decade, but Hokitika was ahead of the times, for in 1866 the *Nelson Examiner* reported: "A theatre is now erecting in

Miss Viola Gillette in A Trip to Chinatown *playing at Dunedin in 1900. (Hocken Library)*

Eugen Sandow, professional strong-man, was a welcome entertainer from overseas. His methods of physical culture spread all over the world. (Alexander Turnbull Library)

Hokitika and will very soon be ready to open . . . Prefabricated in Sydney it is 150 ft by 42 ft. Stairs 7 ft wide, with café, billiards saloon and ladies' refreshment and cloakroom, stage box and four private boxes—nine dressing rooms, green-room with library, wardrobe etc . . . to seat 1,000 . . . A novelty will be the use of gas to light the theatre—the principal chandelier will have thirty-six lights in it, and the effect will be brilliant in the extreme . . . The ceiling is to be of wood, and built in such a manner as to deaden the rattle of rain on the roof, and prevent the performance being disturbed in any weather."

In Napier in the 1880s theatregoers were agog to see their Theatre Royal reopened. Mr E.L. Williams had been paid £100 to construct a new drop curtain and scenery, and a newfangled device had been introduced whereby coloured effects were obtained—low sarsenet screens coloured red or green, fitted in front of the footlights and raised or lowered by the stage manager.

The reopening was a gala occasion, featuring *Called Back*, starring Miss Eloise Juno ("celebrated tragedienne and emotional actress"). Mr C.H. Taylor ("acknowledged to be the best character actor in New Zealand") and Miss Ella Carrington ("from the Queen's and Sadler's Wells theatres, London") supported by a cast of twenty. A waltz specially composed for the occasion was played, the Garrison Band played *Rule Britannia*, and the leading lady orated an Epilogue written by a well-known but anonymous resident.

The smaller country towns were sometimes visited by American cheapjacks, who hired a room and put on a lively but unrefined entertainment for a nominal charge, then raffled and sold "notions" [novelties] to the audience. The author of *Antipodean Notes* described meeting such a showman: "This gentleman travelled in a drag drawn by four fine horses. He was accompanied by Mrs Cheap-jack in a real sealskin jacket, and by two servants in livery, who created a very considerable impression in a colony where the total number of liveried servants could be counted on one's fingers. I overtook his turnout at a roadside inn, and finally left him struggling over a mountain pass, for which his smart carriage was not adapted."

In 1877 the *Auckland Evening Star* reported on an entertainment of much the same type: "Much amusement was created last night in the Albert Hall, in the course of the gift distribution. The professor cried out 'Ninety-five, a bird-cage of the Robinsonian type, walk up for your prize, ticket ninety-five.' A fine young man of graceful manners and polished exterior accordingly walked up the centre of the hall—when a full-blown red crinoline was passed to him, immediately followed by roars of laughter. The young man blushed as he returned with the envied prize, and subsequently it was found under his seat, he had gone home without it."

The Skandinavian Hotel also boasted a concert hall in Invercargill in the 1860s. Note the kerosene lamp and the telegraph lines. By 1866 most of the South Island was linked by telegraph. (Hocken Library)

The country's amateur singers, musicians and aspiring actors sometimes got their hearts' desire when touring companies advertised for local talent to augment cast or orchestra, but otherwise they had to form their own groups. Early in their histories cities, towns and villages set up active dramatic, choral and philharmonic societies.

Amateur dramatic groups were active and there could be little doubt about the plot of a play entitled The Wages of Sin, *or the function of Father's shotgun.*

In 1850, for example the Auckland Amateur Dramatic Society staged a mixed programme in the Military Theatre: "*All at Coventry;* Chinese Dance; Song—*I'm Ninety-Five;* Nigger Song and Dance; concluding with the farce *The Village Lawyers.* (Next month, *High Life Below Stairs.*)"

Audiences were not always noted for their good manners. In 1865 *Dunedin Punch* attended a Philharmonic Society performance: "Admired the fair denizens of the dress circle of course—only, if some of them would not talk quite so loudly next time, Mr Punch would entertain a higher opinion of their—what shall we say?—good taste."

And in Wellington, 1875, the *Evening Post* attended "Lord Lytton's great modern play *Money*" and complained: "The second and third acts were so constantly interrupted by the ill-bred noise, loud talking and vulgar horse-laughs proceeding from one of the boxes that the fine acting was almost lost."

WORDS AND PICTURES

Abraham Lincoln was assassinated on 15 April 1865, but it was not until 9 July of that year that the news reached New Zealand, and then only via a passenger from a passing schooner. Twenty years later the cable via Tasmania was able to bring the London news within only twenty-four hours of despatch.

The daily newspapers of the main centres carried minutely detailed reports of Parliamentary debates, noteworthy sermons by local divines, and social chitchat in an amount of column-space astonishing to present-day readers. The competition between the papers, too, reached heights that they seem too nervous to scale in the 1970s. *The Era* in 1881 took exception to a newly-founded Christchurch paper named *Liberty*: "It is full of nastiness and the most abominable indecency. It clothes the thoughts of a pander in the language of a Fish-Fag. It absolutely bristles with falsehoods, slander, libel, and foul insinuations . . . the outcome of a filthy mind. This Moseley [*Liberty*'s editor] was lately thrashed, kicked, and had two black eyes blackened by some gentleman whom he had slandered. If he ventures to meddle with *The Era* again he is practically certain to come in for another castigating of which he will not rub the marks out in a hurry."

A typical front page, 1865.

Mark Twain, distinguished American humourist, author and lecturer, who visited New Zealand in November 1895, and lectured at the City Hall, Dunedin on "Original Sin" (The Watermelon Story). The front seats were occupied by the Presbyterian and Anglican synods, then sitting in the town. (Canterbury Museum)

Saturday night supplements had popular-magazine value. In 1885 the Wellington *Evening Post* had these treats in store for its readers: "Spirited Away (an original tale)"; "Popping the Question"; "Something About Children"; "Three Africans Cooked in a Gigantic Pie"; "Statistics of Heroes and Heroines"; "Temperance Column"; and "How My Baby Died".

In Dunedin's earliest days Sandy Low, with hand-bell and news-sheet, had publicly cried the news in the streets; but the public should be made to pay for its news, and once a township or even a little fly-by-night goldmining settlement had pitched its tents or huts, a local printer-cum-newspaper proprietor quickly followed. A few of those early local papers have survived until present times to satisfy parish-pump appetites that the big dailies can never meet.

We have elsewhere quoted fairly extensively from their advertising columns, but not from those of the booksellers. "Coffee-table" books were not called by that name, but one can recognise them in: "Drawing Table Books—*Hindostan Illustrated; Mignett's History of the French Revolution; Fischer's Drawing Scrapbook;* also delivered in town—*Christian Witness,* 3d each," (*The New Zealander,* 1880.) By 1885 Alex Sligo of Dunedin was advertising more down-to-earth reading: "*All About Etiquette, Or, The Manners of Polite Society; Young Ladies' Guide to the Work-Table*". And, for more frivolous reading, "*The Canon's Ward* and *Thicker Than Water*".

The novel was at the height of its popularity in the latter half of the nineteenth century, and its writers catered for all tastes. Reading aloud to the family circle was a favourite evening pastime among the upper and middle classes, and the ladies might ply their needles while Papa or some favoured suitor read out Dickens, Thackeray or Trollope. In 1855 Mary Hirst wrote: "I have just

Fires too, were headline news. Dunedin's Princes Street, ravaged by fire in 1865. At this time there was no water supply nor any fire-fighting appliances. (Hocken Library)

Events made news, especially vice-regal occasions. Lord Ranfurly, fifteenth Governor of New Zealand, arrives to open the Mining and Industrial Exhibition in Auckland in 1898. (Auckland Public Library)

Bard, politician and journalist. Thomas Bracken was editor of the Saturday Advertiser *in Dunedin, and his Victorianly sentimental verse became very popular. Under the nom-de-plume of "Paddy Murphy", he wrote the words of* God Defend New Zealand, *a more competent work than most of his poetic output. (Hocken Library)*

"Gem Pocket Library", but more often the stories were designed to appeal to the sighing Cinderella of lonely farmhouse or suburban servant's bedroom; the innocent or humbly-born heroine would be hypnotised by the heir to a peerage and untold millions, the big question being whether he would be a true-blue Gentleman and lead her to the altar, or a whiskered Rat with evil intentions foiled in

Say "good night!" though he be sleeping. List'ning cherubs will be peeping Through God's windows, fondly keeping Loving watch oer Baby.

Sentimental verse was illustrated with splendidly sentimental art. (From Musings in Maoriland)

read *Villette* by Miss Brontë, and am now reading *Westward Ho!*" She goes on to say that there had been a family reading of *Uncle Tom's Cabin* but that poor Father was unwell and had found the story too upsetting.

At a somewhat lower level writers such as Mrs Henry Wood were bestsellers, though her plots were completely predictable and her sweethearts' conversations are incredible today. George Eliot's novels and the Brontë sisters' books were considered dangerous meat for unmarried girls, and the strongest male expletives allowed by publishers were "Pshaw!", "Tcha!" and "Pish!" As the century wore on, and a degrading relaxation set in, stronger words were suggested by dashes; but those writers who had occasion to mention cats and dogs must refer to any poor cat, regardless of sex, as "she", and a dog had to be masculine. The word *bitch* was unthinkable.

At the lowest-price range there were "penny dreadfuls" and "twopenny horribles", catering for the tastes of the *True Confessions* type of thing still popular today. *Done to Death, Or, The Millionaire Heiress* was a title typical of the

Children's books veered from terribly uplifting stories for Sunday reading to fascinating grotesques such as Cole's Funny Picture Book, *an Australian production of 1879 and enormously popular in New Zealand well into the 1920s. Some of the illustrations would make a child-psychologist's hair stand on end.*

The Illustrated London News *and* Pears' Annual *gave away coloured prints of sentimental paintings with their Christmas issues. Thus "Childhood . . . How Little is the happiness that will content a child . . . Clad in rags, and hugging a rag doll, she is yet a princess—nay, a queen, in her own right . . ."* (Hocken Library)

the last chapter by honest Jack Manly, the modest suitor who has worshipped her from afar . . . .

For the male reader there were lurid racing yarns and, in the closing years of the century, elementary thrillers aping the popularity of the *genre* introduced earlier by Wilkie Collins and Dickens, later developed to a higher pitch by Doyle and his inimitable Sherlock Holmes.

By this time magazines such as the *Strand* and the *Illustrated London News* (and its local imitations) had accustomed readers to the pictorial illustration of fact and fancy, and this married up with the appreciation of painting which, for the great majority of middle-class Victorians, meant Landseer and Holman Hunt rather than the incomprehensible decadents such as Manet and, later, Beardsley.

"Every picture tells a story" was a favourite Victorian saying, and if a painting didn't carry a social message, as did Frith's *Derby Day* and Holman Hunt's *Light of the World*, then it was unworthy to grace the walls of the parlour or the drawingroom.

Coloured prints of a sentimental nature—perhaps Millais' *Boyhood of Raleigh* and *Bubbles*—were issued gratis in the Christmas issues of the *Illustrated London News* and were gilt-framed and hung in thousands of New Zealand homes.

In more forward-thinking circles, of course, taste in all the arts was far more sophisticated, but the interested reader must pursue this subject in books specialising in this aspect of period history.

✠ CHURCH AND PEOPLE ✠

Going to church meant more to the Victorian New Zealander than it does to his present-day descendants. Not only was religion taken more seriously, but a great deal of ordinary social life was centred on the church—and attendance at divine service on Sunday mornings and evenings was also an occasion for neighbourly meetings and gossip sessions.

Sermons and services were long, the hard benches made small children wriggle, and as many of the country churches and chapels stood in open paddocks with no friendly bushes to act as comfort stations, we may wonder how such homely matters were managed by the very young and the very old.

Simple piety was the norm and, although sectarian rivalries could become acrimonious, many people had a quite ecumenical outlook. Bernard Chambers of Hawke's Bay, for example, would occasionally attend an Anglican service in the morning and a Presbyterian in the evening, and was in no way put out, when travelling in Australia, to find he was attending a Catholic service by mistake.

As the century progressed there were New Zealand echoes of high-church *versus* low-church among the Anglicans, and there were repercussions of the Darwinian heresy: but by and large the attitude was tolerant. And though the unorthodox evangelic methods of the early Salvation

Army shocked the conventional, to the extent that the Gore Borough Council proposed a bylaw prohibiting the Army's playing or singing on the streets on Sunday, "There was great public opposition to the measure, people branding it as tyrannical and opposed to civil and religious liberty."

The sons and daughters of clergymen were obvious partners in a pious age. Henry Harper of Canterbury and Laura, daughter of the Wanganui missionary-explorer Richard Taylor, were married by him at Putiki in 1859. (Alexander Turnbull Library)

Church picnics were amongst the most important events of the year. The Rev A.J. Reed, on right, dignified in top-hat and binoculars, led his church party to the 854-foot summit of Rangitoto, Auckland's extinct island volcano. This Saturday picnic in 1896 doubtless featured in Sunday's sermon. (A.W. Reed Collection)

Not everyone was punctilious about church-going. One woman writes about her boarder: "He scarcely ever goes to a place of worship, I believe on account of his fits, but he has not had a fit since he lived with us." And a New Zealand bride voyaging across the Pacific, writes: "It is quite a relief not having Sunday today—we have had two together to make up our time properly, and they seemed *long.*"

The Maoris made up for such Pakeha slackness, and in 1860 turned out in force to hear Bishop Williams at Tauranga: "We had a large assembly at church and I was struck, on going towards the building, to see an incredible number of dogs outside, at least a hundred, who had followed their masters."

The Sunday mid-day dinner was by tradition a hot roast, with ample trimmings, and in the afternoon the children might attend Sunday School or indulge in serious Sunday-special reading. Card-playing and secular musicmaking were taboo in many homes, but walking was not ungodly and in Wellington: "Wilkinson's Tea Gardens at Oriental Bay became the popular outing for early settlers. A favourite Sunday afternoon diversion was to stroll round the rocks to the gardens, admire the blooms and hothouses, drink tea in the arbours and chat about the homeland of not too distant memory."

From old letters one gathers that in those days of large families and short lives death was a familiar visitor. A simple and steadfast Christianity was a sure comfort: death was but a calling home to reunion with loved ones who had "gone before", and the date would be sadly but resignedly entered in the big Family Bible.

Mourning clothes, mentioned elsewhere in this book, would be ordered. Black silk could be worn by a widow a year and a day after her husband's demise but it must be trimmed with crape (a black gauze), which could be discarded after eighteen

Many a Victorian child was cautioned by its parent; "Be sure the way you wind about, your sins will always find you out." Here in a Gospel Carriage built by Carter & Carter of Lorne Street, Auckland, itinerant Gospellers entreat the Sinful to listen. (Alexander Turnbull Library)

When doctors mixed their own medicines; when hospitals and nurses did not exist; when antibiotics and analgesics were unheard of, it is no wonder that Death was a frequent visitor. Suitable mourning clothes were a part of every woman's wardrobe. (National Museum)

The Tait Brothers of Auckland were more cheerfully businesslike in 1877: "Cheap Tombstones, Cheap Iron Tomb-Rails. Designs and prices post-free, all work guaranteed. Give us a call before going elsewhere." (*The Evening Star*.)

There was an almost gruesome relish for death. A family in mourning would use black edged notepaper and visiting cards, and Mrs Sherwood's *The Fairchild Family*, judged highly appropriate for children's Sabbath reading, simply wallows in scenes of mortality (some episodes from this book are too macabre even for adults in these days).

And in Hesba Skelton's *The Children of Cloverley*—another most excellent book for the nursery's Sunday reading—Little Annie makes her will, giving her Bible to one little friend, a curl to another, her good clothes must go to her cousins, the shabbier ones to the poor girls in her Sunday-school class. Finally she summons all the household, exhorts them piously and, as the sun rises, expires. Many childish tears must have fallen over these tales, but doubtless there were also juvenile mutineers who decided privately that Little Annie was, simply, a bore.

The churchyard seems a fitting place in which to take leave of our Victorians. Their monuments include Masonic broken columns, funerary urns, weeping angels, clasped hands, fingers pointing heavenwards. Here and there you may still find the remains of immortelles—bunches of metal flowers covered with a glass dome, but some of the graves are marked now only by the "cheap iron tomb-rails" so proudly recommended by the Tait Brothers a hundred years ago.

Emblems of mortality, indeed, on which to close this book.

months, when mauve became permissible. After two years colours might be worn, but many a widow never again wore colours after her bereavement.

A late Victorian fashionable funeral was accompanied by much pomp—black horses and mourning carriages, plumes and so on. In 1860 David Taylor told the public of Dunedin that he had imported " . . . an elegant hearse and other general trappings and would be able to conduct funerals in a manner consonant with the feelings of the bereft".

A final vote of thanks to Mr Bragge and the other photographers of his time, who took pictures of the Victorians for us to look at, and pictures of the Victorians looking at us—here on the Main Street, Masterton. (Alexander Turnbull Library)